JUGGERNAUT

JUGGERNAUT

The Whitman Massacre Trial

1850

RONALD B. LANSING

NINTH JUDICIAL CIRCUIT HISTORICAL SOCIETY

Frontispiece: Oregon City, ca. 1845

The site of the trial, looking east toward the Oregon Trail. The Willamette River is in the foreground, with Mount Hood in the background. The Falls are out of the picture, to the right. Painting by Henry Warre (courtesy Oregon Historical Society).

Library of Congress Cataloging in Publication Data

Lansing, Ronald B.
    Juggernaut : the Whitman Massacre trial, 1850 / Ronald B. Lansing.
        p.   cm.
    Includes bibliographical references and index.
    ISBN 0-9635086-0-1 (paper)
    1. Trials (Murder)—Oregon—Oregon City. 2. Whitman Massacre, 1847. 3. Cayuse Indians—Crime—History. 4. Oregon—History—To 1859. I. Title.
KF223.W46L36   1993
345.795'4102523—dc20   93-16575
[347.9541052523]   CIP

Book design by Corinna Campbell.

Cover illustration: Painting by Henry Warre (courtesy Oregon Historical Society).

To my father and mother,
to their fathers and mothers,
and to all of the old ones from whose *kumtux* and *tseepe*
—wisdom and mistakes—we learn and grow

CONTENTS

ILLUSTRATIONS

PREFACE

In the middle 1800s what became known as the Whitman Massacre shocked the settlers on the Oregon frontier. Much has been written about the massacre and about the life of Marcus Whitman, but little has been written about the trial of the alleged murderers. That trial occurred at Oregon City in the last week of May 1850.

The following account of the trial is told by a fictional narrator who revisits the scene to relive the event. Story telling was an art form prevalent among mountain men, native American Indians, and white settlers on that lonely frontier. For this reason, and in order to provide the reader with a living account and a richer sense of those times, the narrative form and the narrator's patois and idiom have been chosen. Aside from the imagination inherent in all story telling, the facts narrated are authenticated by a careful research of history.

The core of that research lies in four primary authorities, designated as such because they are documents by persons present at the trial who made their reports at the time. These four authorities are:

1. The *Oregon Spectator* article published on May 30, 1850, pp. 2-3 (hereafter cited as *Spectator*, May 30, 1850); see Appendix C.

2. The 1850 Order Book for the United States Court for the County of Clackamas, pp. 16-34 (hereafter cited as 1850 Order Book). This hardbound ledger, prepared by court personnel, was a recording of daily minutes of all official action taken on docketed cases. It is in the Oregon State Archives, Salem, Oregon.

3. A summary transcript of witness testimony and other court rulings at the trial (hereafter cited as Bill of Exceptions). This is a ten-page document, hand-written on the front and back of five sheets of blue stationery (one page blank). It is untitled and informal. It was undoubtedly prepared by one of the defense lawyers and amended by the presiding judge (two additional pages on one sheet), as was required in those days in order to perfect an appeal. It is in the Oregon State Archives, Salem, Oregon; see Appendices A and B.

4. Indictments, summonses, motions, bills, pleas, petitions, verdict, and other papers contained in the file of the case *United States v. Telokite*,

May 1850 (hereafter cited as File, *United States v. Telokite*). It is in the Oregon State Archives, Salem, Oregon.

It is remarkable and fortunate that we have this firsthand documentation available today. These primary authorities provide a well-preserved summary of what transpired at a four-day event that happened a century and a half ago.

To give specificity to this core research, it has been necessary to rely on secondary authority, such as the written reports of witnesses, spectators, survivors, and treatise commentators whose accounts are much removed in time from the trial itself. Furthermore, as with other historians, a certain degree of fair surmise (based upon the author's legal experience) has been used to complete the picture. The footnotes and the narrator's candor will warn the reader when such conjecture is being taken. On the whole, however, the primary authorities form the basis of this work, and are faithfully followed.

The narrator's voice is a diluted version of the syntax, idiom, usages, and vernacular of the Rocky Mountain fur trapper. By the mid-1800s, that patois was encountering the more acceptable English of migrating white settlers. That meeting of language tells us something about a culture clash that was a catalyst for the trial itself. In 1836 Narcissa Whitman wrote to her parents:

> I should like to tell you how the western people talk.... Their language is so singular that I could scarcely understand them, yet it was very amusing. In speaking of quantity, they say "heap of man, heap of water, she is heap sick," etc. If you ask, "How does your wife do today?" "O, she is smartly better, I reckon, but she is powerful weak; she has been mighty bad. What's the matter with your eye?"*

The trial was the Oregon frontier's first attempt to formalize and record judicial proceedings concerning an event of deep and abiding significance to the people of that time. It was a trial that today gives us some insight into the difficult beginnings of formal law, the opening struggles of a new judiciary, and the confrontation of civilizations in a place of wilderness.

Finally, we must never forget that this seminal case represents what is the most critical, the most scrutinized, the most dramatic, the most safeguarded proceeding that takes place in a court of law: the trial of a human being for homicide under penalty of death.

Transactions of the Oregon Pioneer Association, 1891 (Portland, 1893) 86.

ACKNOWLEDGMENTS

This book could not have been written without the help of many. Among those who gave their time were: Paula Abrams, Stephen Dow Beckham, Brian Blum, Colin Dunkeld, James Huffman, Stephen Kanter, Jewel Lansing, George and Joanne Nordling, Terence O'Donnell, Chet Orloff, Kris Olson Rogers, Marjorie Williams Waheneka, and the staffs of the Oregon State Archives, the Oregon Historical Society, the Whitman Mission National Historic Site, and the Lewis and Clark College and Law School libraries. In particular, I would like to thank Philippa Brunsman and Lenair Mulford, whose patience, scrutiny, and industry helped package my words.

Two mass graves in these parts are the spoors of a happening that passed this way upon a time long ago. They are parted by distance but connected by story. One grave is two hundred fifty miles east of here; the other is just down the road somewhere. One has fourteen dead; the other has five. A stone slab marks one; the other is without a marker, so its spot is a mystery. In one, pieces of bodies are buried; whole bodies with roped necks are in the other.

The story of how the first of those mass graves came to be is often told, but not much is said of the second. My name is Eli, and this is my story of that second grave. So put yourself back in those times and at this place.

The sky was gray, and morning had an Oregon mizzle in it. Last evening's rain had made these streets mud. But boot cleaning would not have kept folks away from what was about to happen here on that Tuesday morning so long ago.

Pioneers in that wilderness would gather for just about anything: barn raisings, quilting parties, medicine shows, spelling bees, church picnics, baptisms at the river, or any other excuse to call to mind what they had abandoned far to the east. Fact is, one day, homesick settlers had put down their plows and had come from miles around just to see an apple in Henderson Luelling's orchard. It was the first apple grown on this frontier, and pioneers were drawn to it like starved children.[1]

So the event of this day—a murder trial—was an especially big calling. It was Tuesday morning, the twenty-first day of May in 1850.

I mean to tell you about that murder trial. I was here for it—all four days of it. Court records were kept, and newspaper stories were reported. I have read them all. I was a young man then with an itch and a nose for law doings. What I have to tell you hangs true to a hair and brings you as close as memory allows to what is gone.

The trial happened at this spot, here in the Valley, stuck down on the wet side of the Cascade Mountains. It was then called The Falls, because it was in the mist of that cascade of water over there. Those falls used to run the breadth of the whole Willamette River. Today the spray and sound of that rushing water are blocked out by dams, locks, mills, and other harness. But in those times, when the wind was right, the spray kept things wet even on a sunny day, and the roar sent folks indoors for

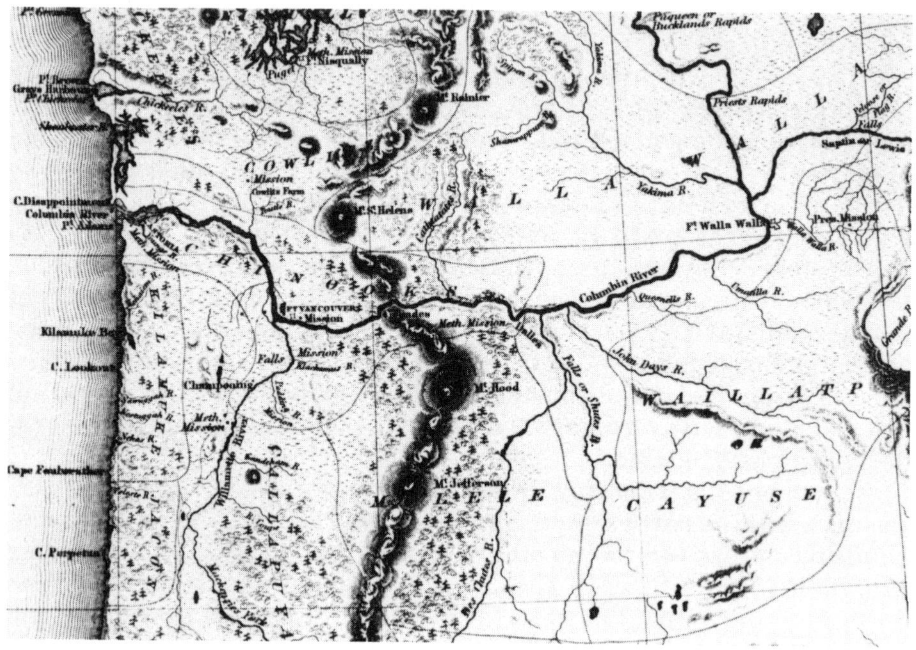

The Oregon Country, ca. 1841

Immigrant settlers used this map in carving the Oregon Trail. The trail entered from the east below the Grande Ronde, proceeded northwest through the Ronde, across Cayuse country by way of either the Umatilla or Walla Walla rivers, then west along the Columbia River to the "Dalles," through the Cascade Mountains to "Ft. Vancouver," and then south to the end of the trail at the "Falls," in the Willamette River valley at the confluence of the "Klackamus R." The town of Oregon City was established at the Falls in 1843. The 1847 massacre took place at the Whitman Mission (Waiilatpu), marked "Pres. [Presbyterian] Mission" on the "Walla Walla R." The 1850 trial took place two hundred miles west, at Oregon City. Map by Charles Wilkes (courtesy Oregon Historical Society).

conversation. The Falls was big medicine to the Indians. *Skookum Chuck* was what they named it—a place of strong water.

For white folks back then, this was a forlorn and formidable place, deep into wild country—two thousand miles and six months of hard travel overland from civilized ways back east. In 1848 this frontier had been made a new territory of the Union. The territory ran from Canada to California and from the Rockies to the Pacific. It was called the Oregon Territory.

In all of that wilderness, there were only nine thousand white souls in 1850. Back then, we banded together around small settlements and felt cheered when we happened on each other's company. It was hard country, and there was much to reckon with—wild critters, cruel weather, hostile Indians, dark forests; but the greatest enemy of all was distance. It was far country and big for loneliness.[2]

The Falls was at center of the Valley settlements. It was the end of the overland wagon trail—a route that people today call the Oregon Trail. The Falls was then the most beautiful place in the Willamette Valley. Some of the settlers were missionaries, some were mountain men, some were retired Hudson's Bay traders, but most were families who had arrived by wagon from the Missouri in the great migrations of the 1840s.

Those pioneers had made a clearing here on the east bank of the Willamette. A town took hold, made up of some five to seven hundred white souls. It was called Oregon City by Doctor John McLoughlin, who had mapped it out. It became the capital city of the territory. There were gristmills and sawmills, some dry-goods stores, a schoolhouse, two churches, a library, and doctor offices. Like that first apple in Luelling's orchard, Oregon City became a small wonder in a big emptiness.

I made home over there across the river on the west bank—a place called Robin's Nest,[3] where some of us old mountain men and our families had come to roost along with what was left of the natives. Before the coming of the white settlers, the Skookum Chuck had been ancient fishing grounds for the Valley Indians.

There had been other murder trials on the Oregon frontier before the one that was to be tried this day. Way back in 1835, Tom Hubbard was brought to trial for killing Thornburgh in a quarrel over a woman. But that was no proper trial. There was no judge and no lawyers; and there was no law or government. Worst of all, there was no chance to spectate. John Townsend, Captain Lambert, and some others got together, made themselves jurymen, gave Hubbard a certificate of innocence, and sent him on his way.[4]

But the proceedings on this Tuesday morning at The Falls was to be a proper trial with official record keeping, full lawyering, and all other trimmings fit for court, just like back east. The people had come west-ward. Here today, their laws followed them.

Two or three hundred settlers left their fields and kitchens to come to the trial. Womenfolk were here as well. Some argued that a woman should stay at home on rainy days, because, when there was mud, a woman had to lift her skirt and the sight of her ankle was not seemly with menfolk around.[5] But manners on a day of this occasion took hind harness. No mud was too deep or dress too high to make a body stay put and miss the show of a murder trial. It was to be an entertainment, a spectacle, a trip to town for those starved by wilderness. Then too, it was a chance to heal an old wound, one that had been festering for two and a half years.

The Morning of the First Day

The trial room was not a true courtroom because the courthouse was not yet built. Sometimes, court had been held outdoors under an oak tree, but this one was not. And there were times when a judge would set shop in someone's log farmhouse, but a cabin would be too small for this crowd. A church room was big enough but not seemly for a murder trial. A schoolroom might have been proper, but school was still in session. None of these were fitting. Rather, this trial took place right over there in a hotel saloon with an upstairs dance hall.[6]

A rail was set across the middle of the room to separate court people from the crowd. Lawyers called that rail a "bar." The railing cut down on places to sit. I came early and had a front seat on a puncheon set on bar-rels by the rail. I sat next to a young man named Anson Cone. Most spec-tators did not have such a good view. They packed in everywhere—along the walls, up and down the stairs. There simply was no room big enough in Oregon City in 1850 for three hundred people. Many of them had to herd around under gray skies.

Chief Tawatoe and some of his Cayuse tribe were among the specta-tors. Tawatoe was called "Young Chief" by the whites. He had been called that since 1830. Here, twenty years later, he was not young anymore.[7] He sat proud and erect, but the other Cayuse were plainly out of sorts. They were a long way from home and were here for two reasons: for one, the five prisoners to be tried were Cayuse; and for another, Gover-nor Lane wanted it so.

That brings us to Lane himself. Sitting there, front-row middle, was the first governor of the whole territory, Joe Lane.[8] He was a busy man. and did not stay long. But he was at court for a purpose: to make certain

Oregon City, ca. 1845

The site of the trial, looking southwest toward the Willamette River Falls. The five Cayuse defendants were imprisoned on the island just below the Falls. This would have been the view of the trail's end for those coming two thousand miles overland by wagon. Painting by John Mix Stanley (courtesy Oregon Historical Society).

Main Street, Oregon City, ca. 1901

The "courtroom" vicinity, showing the McLoughlin house (built in 1846) at its original location on Main Street. The 1850 trial would have been convened in a similar nearby structure, there being no courthouse on the Oregon frontier at the time. (Courtesy Oregon Historical Society.)

that matters commenced to his druthers. This murder trial was most important to the future of the frontier. Lane intended to resign as governor soon, and he desired to leave the territory safe for white settlers. To do that, he wanted the trial to be big medicine about the white man's new order. Seven months before trial, in 1849, he had written:

> The trial and punishments of Indians, in the presence of their tribe and other tribes and bands . . . was the true policy . . . [and] made an impression upon their minds sufficient to deter them from similar offenses.

Lane was of the notion that Indians who killed whites had to be taught a lesson:

> [T]he eyes of the surrounding nations are upon us. . . . [I]f the guilty be not punished, they will construe it as a license for the most atrocious outrages. . . . Cayuse will be incited to gratify any malicious spirit with the blood of Americans. . . . [T]o escape a just punishment, will be to them an appearance of their own safety. Indeed, the chiefs of some of the neighboring tribes . . . have had difficulty in restraining their tribe from joining the Cayuses, and they are anxious the murderes [*sic*] should be brought to punishment, as it would deter their own bands from crime.[9]

Lane's fears of Indian "outrages" and their "malicious spirit" were born of good cause. West of here, in Astoria, just two months before this trial, some Chinooks had killed Bill Stevens. And six months before that, the Snoqualmich had killed Leander Wallace up north in Puget Sound country.[10] Those killings must have weighed heavy on the governor's mind as he waited the start of this murder trial.

But do not think that Lane was a cruel man. He was appointed the Indians' agent as well as the white men's governor and was concerned for both. In a talk to the territory lawmakers, he said that white civilization doomed Indians "to poverty, want and crime." He argued there should be

> "extinguishment of [Indian] title by purchase and locating them in a district removed from the settlements. . . . The cause of humanity calls loudly for their removal from causes and influences so fatal to their existence."[11]

Governor and Indian Agent Lane had two problems, and they ran contrary to each other. He had to head off Indian violence, and that meant swift and open punishment of the killers. But he also had to stop white civilization from destroying the Indians, and that meant letting each go its way. The task was a forked aim that would have set any sharpshooter cross-eyed.

◄〈〈〈 〉〉〉►

Troopers from Company D of Oregon's new Mounted Rifle Regiment came into the courtroom and stood at posts inside the rail, their rifles at ready. It meant the prisoners would soon be arriving. The spectators took note and began to stir. They were anxious to see the faces of the savages that committed the butchery.

The Mounted Rifles were the first troops to enter Oregon Country for military purposes. They had marched two thousand miles on the Overland Trail. It was then the longest march ever made by Union troops and must have been the largest wagon train to cross that trail: three hundred fifty troopers, thirty officers, seven hundred horses, twelve hundred mules, one hundred seventy wagons. They and their dust would have been near three miles long.

In 1847 the Rifles served with honor in the war in Mexico. When those battles were done, they were called here to fight the Cayuse War. In spite of that all, there was no love between the Rifles and the settlers. The troopers stood there facing the crowd, and the crowd sat glaring back. The troops had come to Oregon City just seven months ago and had not been good visitors. Most of them were young recruits far from home and were not happy in this forsaken wilderness. They took to being rowdy and drunk in the streets. A month before trial, seventy of them deserted to the gold in California, and one of their majors tried to cut his own throat while drunk. They even had the poor sense to try to uproot Luelling's apple orchard so as to use it for an arsenal. Some time after the trial, when the Rifles left Oregon City, their abandoned barracks were burnt to the ground by angry settlers.[12]

Marshal Meek brought in the five prisoners. Joseph Lafayette Meek cut a fine figure in his foofaraw of office—a row of shiny brass buttons, a fancy sash, and high collar, all new harness for this newly appointed United States marshal. But those who knew Joe knew that he was no dandy. He had been a Rocky Mountain free trapper in this wilderness long before white settlers came. His outfit for the trial was no more than the revels of a merry mountain man joining into Rendezvous.

The prisoners were dressed in breech clout, fringed leggings, shirts decorated with quill work, moccasins, and pieces of European clothing.[13] They were made to wear more covering than was their custom in late spring. The gentle nature of white women and children needed protection from the naked ways of the first Americans.

Joseph Lane, ca. 1848

The arresting official. The first governor of the Oregon Territory, Lane arranged for the "surrender" of the defendants twenty-nine months after the massacre and twenty months after the United States created the Territory and his office. (Courtesy Oregon Historical Society.)

Joseph L. Meek, ca. 1855 (?)

The court bailiff, who was a United States marshal, a jailer, an executioner, and a mountain man. Meek was also the father of a child who died during the massacre captivity. (Courtesy Oregon Historical Society.)

The crowd studied the prisoners. They were in leg and hand irons, and folks felt better for that. Clokomas was the smallest of the five. Kiamasumkin had a look of wonder as though at any moment he would wake to find himself free again in the mountains. Isiaasheluckas peered from under a bowed head, looking like a wild critter with its foot in the trap. Tomahas had a hard look—long, straight black hair and eyes and mouth squared cruel and cold. He was a big man, like Joe Meek. Chief Telokite was wrinkled and grayed by years and by the troubles of a leadership that had finally come to reckoning.[14] When the prisoners saw Young Chief Tawatoe and the other Cayuse in the crowd, they were steadied by it.

In 1849 Governor Lane described the Cayuse as a "haughty, proud, overbearing people . . . very superstitious . . . well armed, [who] are, through fear, on amicable terms with the whites." But in 1839 a man of learning named John Kirk Townsend had seen the Cayuse differently. He said, "I have never seen a race of people who appeared more shrewd and intelligent . . . a noble looking race."[15] The ten years between the two reports tells the difference. The stream of white immigrants increased steadily between 1839 and 1849, and that changed both white and Cayuse hearts.

Here in Oregon City on this day, the Cayuse were far from their hunting grounds. They had come a long way from the other side of the Cascade Mountains, two hundred fifty miles east by horse, two hundred miles as geese go. They were easy to separate from the native Valley Indians. The Cayuse rode tall, but the Valley Indians had lost their leaders and had come to live off of the white man. Valley Indians threw a weak shadow and were a sorrow to see.

A year before trial, Lane had reported that there were about eight hundred Cayuse souls. There was no way to know a fact like that for certain. It was all just eye-balling. A year after this trial, a census taker said there were only 120 Cayuse.[16] It could be they were both right, because much had happened to the Cayuse nation in the two years between the two reports.

No doubt the Cayuse were a cantankerous people, especially compared with the Nez Perce, their neighbors, a more peace-loving tribe. Maybe the attitudes of those tribes might have been different if their hunting grounds had been reversed. The Nez Perce territory was far to the north and east of the white immigrants' Overland Trail, but Cayuse land was cut down the middle by that passage. In 1843 some nine hundred *shuyapu* came overland. *Shuyapu* is an Indian word for white folks. In 1844 twelve hundred more *shuyapu* were seen along the trail. In 1845 three thousand came. By 1847 the Cayuse watched forty-five hundred settlers cross their hunting grounds.[17] On and on they came from out of the Snake River Valley, through the Blue Mountains, across the plateau, and on out the Columbia River Gorge to the Valley. The *shuyapu* were bringing their wagons and plows and horses and cattle; but more than those belongings, they were bringing disease and yearnings for land.

Meek brought his five prisoners from the jail on Abernethy Island at the foot of the Falls. A bridge joined the island to the east bank of the Willamette River. Cayuse did not understand jails and called them *skookum* houses.[18]

Three weeks before trial, Governor Lane and the Mounted Rifle Regiment had brought the prisoners in from The Dalles—a fort and mission one hundred miles east of The Falls on the other side of the Cascade Mountains. At The Dalles, Young Chief and the Cayuse nation surrendered the prisoners to Lane in late April and early May. Lane had been working for that delivery as far back as November 1849.

Lane did not approve of the way the Oregon Volunteer troops tried to bring in the murderers. In the spring of 1848, before Lane and the Mounted Rifles came to Oregon, the volunteer troops had ponied up wheat, blankets, shirts, and other reward for any Indian who would capture and deliver the murderers. Lane thought poorly of that tactic. He felt that when a mule was haunched down, it was a stick, not a carrot, that got it pulling again.[19]

So, in November 1849, Lane steered a different course. He did it all with pen and paper. He sent courier letters to the Nez Perce chiefs, to Young Chief Tawatoe, to William McBean of the Hudson's Bay post at Fort Walla Walla, to William Craig, and to Major Hathaway of the Mounted Rifles. He urged the Nez Perce not to join with the Cayuse. He talked peace to the Cayuse but demanded to have the murderers. He called Young Chief and the Cayuse nation "friends," but he said there would be war if the murderers were not given over. With the help of McBean, Lane was able to give the names of the suspected killers. The governor got what he wanted. The Cayuse and the Nez Perce went off into the Blue Mountains after Telokite and his renegade band.

After months of chase and starvation, Telokite and the other four prisoners were talked into surrender. Then Young Chief Tawatoe, his warriors, and the prisoners made the hundred-fifty-mile ride west to The Dalles and to the rendezvous with Lane. The prisoners were handed over.[20]

It was not clear what was meant by this delivery. Were the Cayuse saying these were murderers? Or were they just smoking peace with the governor by giving him the braves he named? The meaning of that rendezvous in The Dalles was to become a big turn in the trial doings.

So here sat the five prisoners, wrapped around by the stares and murmurs of the crowd. They were two hundred fifty miles from their native land in the ryegrass of eastern Oregon. They sat quiet in a room that barely ten years before had been a patch of meadow in the wild country of their cousin tribes.

Then into the room came a heap of court people: the clerk, his deputy, the lawyers, the United States attorney, and interpreters. They went straight to their positions and made ready for the arrival of the judge.

Court Clerk George Curry sat down at a table piled with books and papers, took off his coat and high hat, rolled up his shirtsleeves, and went to work. He was a likeable man and was headed to be governor of the Territory in a few years. But he was not ambitious for politics, as many had come to be now that government had come to Oregon. He was a man of letters who had edited and published newspapers. Lawmakers often called on him to phrase a proclamation. But for now, he was just a clerk, and a reluctant one at that. Last Christmas he gave up his clerk job so that he could retire to farming outside of town. But for this important trial, Curry had been pressed back into clerk service. Later I will have to say more about the reason for that.[21]

At Curry's side was Frank Holland, deputy clerk. Holland was scribe for the doings. In his hand and through his eyes and ears the court's 1850 Order Book was written. That ledger recorded the decisions and orders made at trial.

There was also a curious-looking man who took a seat off in a corner near the bench. Every day of the trial he would busy himself with pen and paper. Turns out that he was the reporter from the *Oregon Spectator*—the first and only newspaper on the frontier. One week after the trial this reporter's story was published. It began:

> [W]e give below, a minute and careful report, which we prepared ourself, expressly for the Spectator. If we do not always express ourself with legal precision, our legal friends will kindly keep in mind that we are wholly un-used to legal proceedings. Our report, as to the facts of it, may be relied on as minute and faithful. And we here ten-der our respectful acknowledgements to Judge Pratt for his kindness in permitting us to occupy a seat within the bar, for the purpose of taking down the proceedings of Court.[22]

Two tables were spaced apart in front of the bench. They were the lawyer tables. Ten souls crowded around one of them: five prisoners, three defense lawyers, and two interpreters.

Two interpreters were needed because three languages would be spoken at trial: English, Cayuse, and the Jargon. Few of the tribes in the Territory spoke the same tongue. Save for signs, most could not understand one another. The Cayuse and the Nez Perce had come to have the same speech, but they could not understand the Paiute. The Paiute could not understand the Rogue River tribes, and those tribes could not understand the Kalapuya. And none of them could understand the Shoshoni. So, long before white pioneers came, the tribes worked out a language for trade so they could do business. It was called the Chinook Jargon. Many of the early white traders and settlers picked up on the Jargon. But the Cayuse were a people who kept to themselves, and many of them were not so ready to use the Jargon. That meant that when white man's English was spoken at trial, one of the interpreters had to translate it into the Jargon, so that the other interpreter could go from Jargon to the Cayuse-Nez Perce tongue. When Cayuse was spoken, the interpreters came back the other direction. It meant that talk had to play out three times before it reached target.[23]

At the other lawyer table sat one body—Amory Holbrook, the prosecutor. President Polk appointed Holbrook to be the United States attorney for the Oregon Territory. Unlike Curry, Holbrook was very political, one of those who measured life by who to pack with and who to ride against. He tasted of power, policy, and patriotism; went against Catholics and foreigners; and favored the notions of a secret group called the Supreme Order of the Star-Spangled Banner, an organization that folks called the "Know-Nothings" because members would claim ignorance of its doings.[24]

Holbrook got himself and Marshal Meek into trouble a few months after trial. They were suspected of making off with $40,000 of public money—money received from the sale of a ship, the *Albin*, at public auction. Some said it was no more than $1,450 and that Meek had nothing to do with it. Whatever the amount and whoever the culprit, no charges were ever brought.[25]

All were now in place except for His Honor. That entrance received special ceremony. Mountain man Marshal Meek bellowed out in his best auctioneer voice, "All get up! This court is now in meeting! Judge Pratt in charge!"

It was loud, and folks leaped to their feet like ducks from a pond at gunshot. It was no wonder that pioneers at Champoeg back in 1843 voted to form a government; Meek was there, and when he yelled out, "All in favor of . . . an organization, follow me!,"[26] voters probably stepped to his side more out of jerk than judgment.

With everyone stood proper, Judge Orville C. Pratt, associate justice for the Territory of Oregon, entered the makeshift courtroom at the hour of nine on the forenoon of Tuesday, May 21, 1850. He went to the bench— another table at the center of the back wall. He stood looking over the

Orville C. Pratt, ca. 1870s (?)

The trial judge, who was also a businessman, a politician, and a millionaire. (Courtesy Oregon Historical Society.)

Amory Holbrook, ca. 1860s (?)

The prosecutor. Holbrook was a United States attorney and a member of the Supreme Order of the Star-Spangled Banner. (Courtesy Oregon Historical Society.)

crowd, all standing. Then he pointed his gavel at the Cayuse. They were still seated. It was no disrespect. The interpreters forgot to tell them what Meek's yelling was about.

When the Cayuse finally rose, the judge sat; and then so sat everyone except the Cayuse, who had to be told to sit no sooner than they had stood. This custom of sitting and standing must have been a wonder to Indians. It must have been twice a wonder when it forced older chiefs like Telokite, Tawatoe, and Governor Lane to rise for the coming of this younger man. Judge Pratt was only thirty years of age. *Hyas tyees* do not pay honor to a *tyee*—just as the *Saghalie Tyee* would never pay honor to a *hyas tyee*.[27]

His Honor was an easterner new to the frontier. He had read and practiced law in New York and Illinois and had been sent by President Polk to Oregon to be judge when the Territory formed. He had been holding court on the frontier for just the last nine months.[28]

He was a man of dignity and airs and was given to the gavel. His power in court was like a quirt he took to using many times. Those who were in contempt of him were quick to be fined or jailed. Lawyers, witnesses, jurors, even Marshal Meek had been punished for not being serious about circumstance owed the court.[29]

Pratt's body was ample but, on this day, was hidden by a black robe that he borrowed from some reverend for this special trial. Likely, the Cayuse were not impressed by the judge's rig-out and finery. It was somber and without color. Like missionary garb, it had no quills, beads, feathers, or other foofaraw fit for a *tyee*.[30]

Aside from his judge job, Pratt was also a clever businessman. He traded in stoves, blankets, boots, lumber, and other such needs of frontier life. His judicial salary was $2,000 a year, but he ended life a millionaire. He was also active in Territory politics.[31]

Here was a man who put a nose and finger to the winds of business and government. Those winds were all about in the trial now before him. Governor Lane had strong feelings about how this case should come to end. And the new pioneers had feelings as well—feelings about "Injuns," Catholics, Bay Company foreigners, and the backwoods manners of a frontier with its mountain men, their squaws, and unrefined living. These were of no matter to blind justice, but Pratt was not a man to grope blindfolded.

Folks saw Pratt's conduct at this trial in different ways. The *Spectator* reporter wrote that there was a "universal feeling of admiration [for] . . . the energy, firmness, and enlightened prudence with which the judge conducted this trial." But Elam Young wrote that Pratt's "moral character stands very low here, it otto be rubbed up a little."[32]

His Honor began the proceedings by asking the United States attorney if he had any business for the court. Of course, Pratt knew good and well what was in store, but the asking was all part of the ceremony. Things were to be done proper at this trial, just like back east.

Holbrook stood and said he had a grand jury indictment. "Indictment Number Eleven: United States versus Telokite *et al.*" The *et al.* part meant the other four defendants.

Pratt said to get on with it.

So Holbrook made a nod to Clerk Curry, and Curry nudged Deputy Clerk Frank Holland, who then got up and commenced to read the indictment:[33]

> "At a District Court of the United States of America, for the District of Oregon [County of Clackamas], begun and holden at Oregon City in said county within and for said District, on the thirteenth day of May in the year of our Lord one thousand eight hundred and fifty.

> "The Jurors of the United States, within and for said District, on their oath present:

> "That on the twenty ninth day of November in the year of our Lord one thousand eight hundred and forty seven, at Wai-il-at-pu, in said county, the said place being then and there in the Indian country, certain Indians named Telakite, Tomahas otherwise called the Murderer, Clok-omas, Isiaasheluckas and Kiamasumkin, with certain other Indians whose names are to the Jurors unknown, with force and arms in and upon one Marcus Whitman, the said Whitman not then and there being an Indian, did make an assault."

Holland was not yet finished reading, not by a far shot. The indictment went on and on in fancy form and lawyer words that measured twenty inches of paper in seventy lines of fine script. Behind Holland's reading was the murmur of the interpreters trying to translate: "*Kopa skookum pe muskets saghalie kopa Marcus Whitman, yaka halo siwash, mamook pight elip. . . .* " The interpreters were trying to keep up, but no translator could put that King's English into Cayuse-Nez Perce tongue or Chinook Jargon.

Holland kept on reading. Defendants assaulted Whitman with

> "certain guns, muskets and pistols, each of the same then and there being loaded and charged with gunpowder and bullets, which guns . . . the said Indians in their hands then and there had and held, to, against and upon the

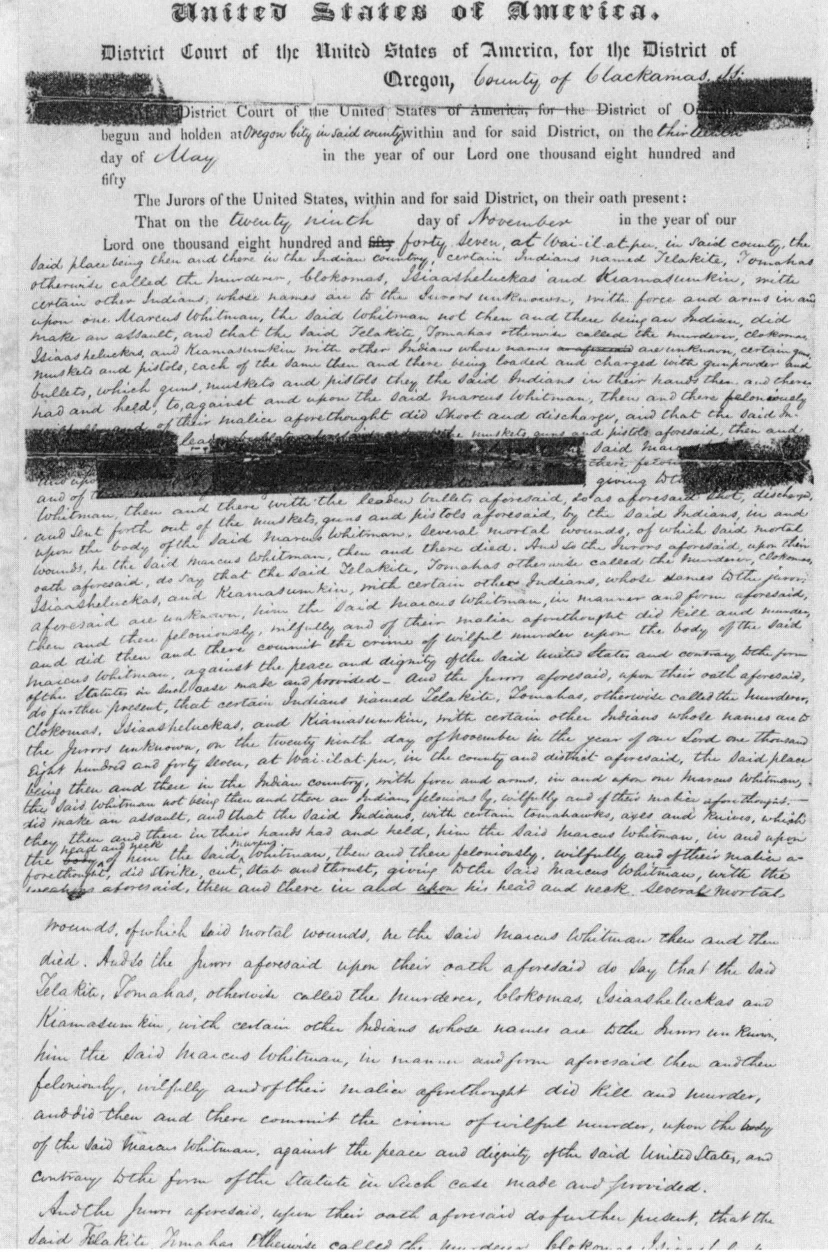

United States of America.

District Court of the United States of America, for the District of

Oregon, *County of Clackamas*.

~~District Court of the United States of America, for the District of Oregon~~

begun and holden at *Oregon City in said county* within and for said District, on the *thirteenth*

day of *May* in the year of our Lord one thousand eight hundred and

fifty

The Jurors of the United States, within and for said District, on their oath present:

That on the *twenty ninth* day of *November* in the year of our

Lord one thousand eight hundred and ~~fifty~~ *forty Seven*, at Wai-il-at-pu, in said county, the said place being then and there in the Indian country, certain Indians named Telakite, Tomahas otherwise called the murderer, Clokomas, Isiaasheluckas and Kiamasumkin, with certain other Indians, whose names are to the Jurors unknown, with force and arms in and upon one Marcus Whitman, the said Whitman not then and there being an Indian, did make an assault, and that the said Telakite, Tomahas otherwise called the murderer, Clokomas, Isiaasheluckas, and Kiamasumkin with other Indians whose names are ~~unknown~~ unknown, certain guns, muskets and pistols, each of the same then and there being loaded and charged with gunpowder and bullets, which guns, muskets and pistols they the said Indians in their hands then and there had and held, to, against and upon the said Marcus Whitman, then and there feloniously

... of their malice aforethought did shoot and discharge, and that the said M...

... the muskets guns and pistols aforesaid, then and ... said Ma...

... their felon...
... giving to the...

and of the...

Whitman, then and there with the leaden bullets aforesaid, so as aforesaid, shot, discharged and sent forth out of the muskets, guns and pistols aforesaid, by the said Indians, in and upon the body of the said Marcus Whitman, Several mortal wounds, of which said mortal wounds, he the said Marcus Whitman, then and there died. And so the Jurors aforesaid, upon their oath aforesaid, do say that the said Telakite, Tomahas otherwise called the murderer, Clokomas, Isiaasheluckas, and Kiamasumkin, with certain other Indians, whose names to the jurors aforesaid are unknown, him the said Marcus Whitman, in manner and form aforesaid, then and there feloniously, wilfully and of their malice aforethought did kill and murder, and did then and there commit the crime of wilful murder upon the body of the said Marcus Whitman, against the peace and dignity of the said United States and contrary to the form of the Statutes in such case made and provided — And the jurors aforesaid, upon their oath aforesaid, do further present, that certain Indians named Telakite, Tomahas, otherwise called the murderer, Clokomas, Isiaasheluckas, and Kiamasumkin, with certain other Indians whose names are to the Jurors unknown, on the twenty ninth day of November in the year of our Lord one thousand eight hundred and forty Seven, at Wai-il-at-pu, in the county and district aforesaid, the said place being then and there in the Indian country, with force and arms, in and upon one Marcus Whitman, the said Whitman not being then and there an Indian, feloniously, wilfully and of their malice aforethought, did make an assault, and that the said Indians, with certain tomahawks, axes and knives, which they then and there in their hands had and held, him the said Marcus Whitman, in and upon the head and neck the said Whitman, then and there feloniously, wilfully and of their malice aforethought, did strike, cut, stab and thrust, giving to the said Marcus Whitman, with the weapons aforesaid, then and there in and upon his head and neck, Several mortal

wounds, of which said mortal wounds, he the said Marcus Whitman then and there died. And so the jurors aforesaid upon their oath aforesaid do say that the said Telakite, Tomahas, otherwise called the murderer, Clokomas, Isiaasheluckas and Kiamasumkin, with certain other Indians whose names are to the jurors unknown, him the said Marcus Whitman, in manner and form aforesaid then and then feloniously, wilfully and of their malice aforethought did kill and murder, and did then and there commit the crime of wilful murder, upon the body of the said Marcus Whitman, against the peace and dignity of the said United States, and contrary to the form of the Statute in such case made and provided.

And the jurors aforesaid, upon their oath aforesaid do further present, that the said Telakite, Tomahas otherwise called the murderer, Clokomas, Isiaasheluckas ...

Grand Jury Indictment

A portion of the first page of Indictment Number Eleven, dated May 13, 1850, charging the five defendants with murder and alleging Marcus Whitman to be the victim. Although there were other indictments for other alleged massacre victims, the trial concerned this indictment and this victim and no other. (Courtesy Oregon State Archives, Clackamas County, U.S. District Court Records.)

said Marcus Whitman . . . [and] feloniously, wilfully and
of their malice aforethought did shoot and discharge . . .
the leaden bullets aforesaid out of the muskets . . . aforesaid . . . in and upon the body of him the said Marcus
Whitman . . . [and] did strike, penetrate, and wound, giving to the said Marcus Whitman . . . several mortal
wounds, of which said mortal wounds, he the said Marcus Whitman then and there died."

Put short and simple, the indictment charged that defendants shot and
killed Whitman.

But that was still not the end of it. The indictment went on and re-
peated the same words, only this time saying that the killing was done by
"tomahawks, axes and knives," instead of "guns, muskets, and pistols."
Then, as if those were not enough ways to kill, the indictment said it all
a third time, this time saying the killing happened "in some way and
manner . . . to the jurors aforesaid unknown."

So, in full flower, the grand jury and Prosecutor Holbrook claimed that
Whitman was murdered by bullets or blades or whatever. From the witnesses heard, the grand jury felt that Holbrook had evidence that Whitman was killed and that the prisoners did it, but that there was uncertain
evidence as to how it was done.[34]

The indictment called off the names of all five defendants at least six
times: "Telakite, Tomahas otherwise called the Murderer, Clokomas,
Isiaasheluckas and Kiamasumkin." Throughout the trial, whenever that
roster was called, Tomahas was branded "the Murderer." In a trial set to
decide if Tomahas was a murderer, it was no help to his cause to be
named as such. It was a name given him by his own tribe long before
the Whitman killing.[35]

The indictment put the date of the killing on November 29, 1847. That
was two and one-half years before trial. Witness memories would be
dimmed by that passing of time.

The indictment called the place of the killing Waiilatpu. In Cayuse-
Nez Perce tongue, *Waiilat* means the Place of Ryegrass. When *-pu* is put
to the end of a word, it means "the people of that place." In English, we
say Oregon is the place, but we add letters making it *Oregonian* when we
mean a person from Oregon. The Cayuse did the same. So *Waiilatpu*
were the People That Lived at the Place of Ryegrass.[36] But to all of the
white settlers in the Valley, Waiilatpu was known as a place, not a people.
It had come to be a name for the Whitman Mission—not the name of the
original souls and not the name of their native place.

That little *-pu* ending meant even more. It was big medicine—a sign of
the difference in how the first Americans and the white settlers looked at
landowning. Indians thought of people as belonging to the land: people

of the ryegrass, not the ryegrass of the people. It is not the land of yours or of mine; instead, we are all *of the land.*

Marcus Whitman was a Protestant missionary doctor who had settled his mission at Waiilatpu way back in 1836. He and his missus, Narcissa, made it their work to tend the Christian and medicine needs of the Cayuse Indians.

For the first six years, Waiilatpu served as a true mission tending the Cayuse needs. But early in the 1840s, wagon wheels began to carve their overland ruts. This Overland Trail ran close to Waiilatpu and made the mission a stopping place for the caravans. It was a final station to rest up from the hard and cruel Snake River and Blue Mountains crossing and to make ready for the final push through the Columbia Gorge and Cascade Mountains before reaching journey's end in the Valley.

The hospitality, medicine, and spirit comfort of Waiilatpu had been a special welcome to the sick, the lame, and those too tired to go on. So many families used the Mission House as a resting place that Whitman built a separate building, the Mansion House, to board his tired countrymen. Besides being a doctor and missionary to the Cayuse, Whitman was becoming a patriot who fancied seeing the American settlement of Oregon.

In the spring of 1844, when last I had talked to Doctor Whitman at Waiilatpu, I asked him what he made of the rise of immigrants coming into Oregon Country. He said, "Our greatest work is . . . to aid the white settlement of this country and help . . . its religious institutions."

I wondered how that squared with his mission work for the Cayuse. He said that there would not be time for Indian progress because "the white settlers will demand the soil and seek the removal of both the Indians and the mission; what Americans desire of this kind, they always effect."

I saw in that a powerful sorrow. But he said that if the Indians "refuse or neglect to fill the designs of Providence, they ought not to complain" and Christians ought not "to be anxious on their account."

I scratched my head and asked to know more about this Providence and how it was Christian. He said that the Indians had not "obeyed the command to multiply and replenish the earth," and that they could not "stand in the way of others doing so."

That was the last I ever saw of Doctor Whitman. So for me, those were his parting words—words by which he lived and, as things turned out, words by which he died.[37]

Waiilatpu had also been an orphanage. The long trip overland from the Missouri left children without parents, and wagon masters would drop the orphans off at the mission. The half-breed children of mountain men were also left there because the rigors of trapper life were not suited to child-rearing. At the time of the killing, the mission had housed thirteen orphans, including seven Sager family children and the métis

Marcus and Narcissa Whitman, ca. 1847

No other first-hand likenesses of the Whitmans are known to exist. These sketches are believed to have been made by the artist Paul Kane four months before the couple's deaths. The authenticity of the sketches has been substantially verified by the late Clifford M. Drury, the leading biographer of the Whitmans. (Courtesy Royal Ontario Museum, Toronto.)

daughters of mountain men Jim Bridger and Joe Meek. The total population at the mission was seventy-five, including ten families, six bachelors, plus Marcus Whitman and his missus. Except for seven métis, the seventy-five were all white.[38]

That population did not count the Cayuse who had made camp close by. The Cayuse spread their camps across their vast hunting grounds. Other camps led by Chiefs Stickus, Camaspelo, Young Chief, and Five Crows were many miles from the mission. The Cayuse camp at the mission was led by Chief Telokite.

The closest white folks were at Fort Walla Walla, a Hudson's Bay trading post twenty miles west. Fifty miles south was a Catholic mission. Whitman's fellow Protestant, Reverend Henry Spalding, had a mission at Lapwai among the Nez Perce seventy miles east. There was another Protestant mission one hundred miles north. Those were the closest neighbors. The nearest city was here at The Falls, two hundred fifty miles west.

Of course, Cayuse country was surrounded by the hunting grounds of other tribes. The Walla Walla were west, the Umatilla south, the Paiute further down in the Basin, the Shoshoni south and east over by the Snake River, the Nez Perce east, the Palouse north, the Yakima north and west.[39]

The Cayuse were the orneriest of the lot. As Governor Lane had said, they were a "proud, haughty, overbearing" people. Long before the white man came, Cayuse called themselves *Te-taw-ken*, a name that meant "superior people." Then came the Canadian trappers and called them *Cailloux*, a French word that meant "rock people." Americans got hold of that French word and spelled it C-a-y-u-s-e.[40] It seemed like everyone had a thing to say for the Cayuse except the Cayuse themselves. Matters were no different at the murder trial.

By and by, Frank Holland got to the bottom of his indictment reading:

> "said Indians . . . did commit the crime of wilful murder
> in and upon the body of said Marcus Whitman, against
> the peace and dignity of the United States aforesaid, and
> contrary to the form of the Statute in such case made and
> provided."

It has never been clear just what "Statute" the killing was contrary to. It might have been Elijah White's code of laws or, maybe, the *Little Bluebook* or, maybe, the *Big Bluebook*. No one ever drew a bead on that. The stream of criminal laws at that time was fed by many forks.

In 1842 the American government back in Washington City had appointed Elijah White to be the Indian agent for this area. At that time, he had come out to Lapwai and pow-wowed with some Nez Perce chiefs and with Chief Five Crows of the Cayuse. Reverend Spalding, Tom McKay, and British agents from the Hudson Bay Company had been there as well. Spalding and White were set on getting the Indians to agree to some written rules of manners. Indians had a way of thieving and trespassing without getting fixed punishment. When tribal punishment was given, it was a punishment too soft to satisfy Spalding's and White's notions. Indians in northwest California would punish a murderer by a fine of fifteen or ten dentalium strings. If the killer refused to pay, then he would be made a slave. If he refused to be a slave, then he could be killed.[41]

So, in the early 1840s, Indian Agent White got the chiefs to agree to a code of eleven written articles. Article One said: "Whoever wilfully takes life shall be hung." Article Eleven said: "If any Indian break these laws, he shall be punished by his chiefs, if a white man breaks them, he shall be reported to the agent, and be punished at his instance."[42]

Those articles were not likely to be the "Statute" mentioned in the indictment. For one, White had no power to make such a treaty. For another, the articles plainly stated that the chiefs punished Indians; Pratt and this *shuyapu* court had no such power. If a statute was violated, it would have to be something other than the Elijah White Code.

While White was busy trying to make order for the Indians, settlers here in the Valley had begun to do the same for themselves. As far back as 1841 both British and American citizens wanted some organization in this lawless place. But it was not until July 5, 1843, that a makeshift government took hold at Champoeg, a place upriver from The Falls. "Provisional organization," it was called. Those who took part in the Champoeg meetings were farmers and shop owners who had no time or wish to go through argument or rule-making on all sorts of crime and other matters fit for government. In those days, it was faster to stick to an old and winding deer path than to bushwhack a new trail. So Jim O'Neil brought out a book called the 1839 *Statute Laws of the Territory of Iowa*. O'Neil said, "Let's just adopt this." That idea fit everyone's druthers.

Law books were scarce on this frontier in 1843, so the citizen lawmakers paid O'Neil $10.50 for that Iowa book and two others that he had. Then they voted and passed laws of organization; the "Organic Law" of the Oregon Provisional Government, it was called. Article Twelve of that Organic Law said this:

> The statutes of Iowa territory shall be the law of this territory in civil, military, and criminal cases, in all cases not otherwise provided for, and where no provision of

> said statutes applies the principles of common law and
> equity shall govern.

O'Neil's Iowa statute book became Oregon law and was called the "Bluebook" because of its color. Under the chapter on Crimes and Punishments, the *Bluebook* said:

> Sec. 1. Murder shall consist in the unlawful killing of a human being in the peace of the United States, with malice aforethought either expressed or implied. . . .

> Sec. 2. . . . The punishment of any person convicted of the crime of murder shall be death.[43]

After 1843, more and more wagons had come to the Valley, and these new settlers had their own notions about law. Pioneer lawmakers got together again in 1844 and 1845 to put more teeth to the rules. They made some changes in the Organic Law and left out the part about adopting Iowa Territory statutes. Still, it seemed to be understood that the Iowa *Bluebook* would govern crime on this frontier.

That was the lay of white man's law on November 29, 1847, the day Whitman was killed. But could those Organic Laws have any power over Indians? The Preamble to the 1845 Organic Law read: "We, the people of Oregon Territory . . . agree to adopt the following laws and regulations until such time as the United States of America extend their jurisdiction over us." Indians had no part in that agreement, and they most certainly were not inviting the Union to "extend their jurisdiction over us." Article One, Section 3, of that Organic Law said this about the first Americans:

> The utmost good faith shall always be observed towards the Indians; . . . and in their property, rights and liberty, they shall never be invaded or disturbed, unless in just and lawful wars . . .; but laws founded in justice and humanity, shall, from time to time, be made for preventing injustice being done to them, and for preserving peace and friendship with them.

This murder trial was surely headed toward a disturbance of their liberty, and was surely not apt to preserve peace and friendship with them. As to Indians, the Provisional Government was on loose slope.

In the two and one-half years between the killing and this murder trial, lawmaking got even more bothered. Back in Washington City, in August 1848, Congress had passed a law making Oregon an official United States Territory. When word of that reached Oregon in March

1849, that brought the doings of the Provisional Government to an end but kept alive some of its laws. The Territory Act said:

> Section 14. . . . [T]he existing laws now in force in the territory of Oregon, under the authority of the provisional government . . . , shall continue to be valid and operative. . . .

> Section 17. . . . [A]ll crimes . . . against the laws in force within said limits, may be prosecuted, tried, and punished in the courts established by this act.[44]

The idea was simple enough: No one reckoned to lose the horse while passing the reins. It meant that the 1839 Iowa *Bluebook* was still good law in the new Territory.

But then in September 1849, just eight months before this trial, the new Territorial Legislature met for more lawmaking. Many of the old Provisional lawmakers had gone back to their crops and animals. The new Territorial lawmakers had an eye for item and brains for threadwork, and they commenced to stitch up loose ends. A lawyer named William Chapman urged the lawmakers to adopt the new Iowa Statutes. He had been a lawyer in Iowa and reported that the Iowa Territory had passed fresh laws in 1843. He then produced a copy of the *Revised Statutes of Iowa of 1843*. It was blue-colored, just like the 1839 Iowa Statutes, only it was thicker by a quarter of an inch. So it was called the *Big Bluebook* while the old Iowa Statute book was called the *Little Bluebook*.[45]

The Oregon Territorial Legislature adopted the whole of the *Big Bluebook* in one vote. That was the rub. Some argued, including Attorney General Holbrook, that the *Big Bluebook* was illegal because it was passed in one lump instead of in parts. Holbrook called it a "steamboat code" because it carried so many different cargoes in one passage. Section 6 of the Territorial Act of Congress said:

> To avoid improper influences, which may result from intermixing in one and the same act such things as have no proper relation to each other, every law shall embrace but one object, and that shall be expressed in the title.

Holbrook said that the *Little Bluebook* was still law and the *Big Bluebook* was not.

Judge Pratt had a different notion. Pratt took the position in private that the Territorial Legislature had the power to do what it did and that the *Big Bluebook* was the law. That made a strange predicament for this

Cayuse murder trial. Prosecutor Holbrook fixed to practice out of one set of laws and Judge Pratt out of another.

But that was not the only ruckus. By May of 1850, Oregon lawmakers had been passing laws, amending some, and abolishing others for a period of seven years. Not one of them had been printed up or made available to the people. It was all just a heap of handwritten acts and minutes spread out among different record keepers. Someone was needed to sort through it all, to put the laws in order, and to publish them in an organized fashion. So two weeks before the trial, the Territorial Legislature had given that job to George Curry and William Buck.

It was no small task, and Curry and Buck had to dig around and find all of those handwritten papers and the laws adopted. There were only two copies of the *Big Bluebook* and four of the *Little Bluebook* in the whole Territory. Not long after the trial, Curry and Buck published their work in a handbook called the "Twenty Acts," but at the time of trial they had only got as far as collecting their materials.

That was probably the reason why Curry was called back to duty as court clerk. He was there to help resolve differences between a judge who followed the *Big Bluebook* and a prosecutor who followed the *Little Bluebook*. Curry had gathered up the laws. He was the court's only law library.[46] His folks must have seen the coming. They gave him the middle name *Law*—George Law Curry.

As Deputy Holland stood there rambling off that long indictment of Prosecutor Holbrook's, a piece of the difference between the two *Bluebooks* cut through. The murder statute in the *Little Bluebook* under Crimes and Punishments said:

> Sec. 1. . . . The unlawful killing may be perpetrated by poisoning, starving, drowning, stabbing, shooting, or by any other of the various forms or means by which human nature may be overcome and death thereby occasioned.

But the *Big Bluebook* said:

> Sec. 2. The manner of the killing is not material.[47]

Back in the Iowa Territory, its Supreme Court had praised the reform that simplified indictments:

> There is now a prevailing tendency to simplify legal proceedings, by divesting them of superfluous verbiage and useless repetitions, which can only serve to present the crime so charged in awful sound and form.[48]

George Law Curry, ca. 1855
The clerk of the court was a compiler of laws, a farmer, a "law librarian," and
a future governor of the Oregon Territory. (Courtesy Oregon Historical Society.)

But Holbrook, feeling that the *Little Bluebook* was still the law in the Oregon Territory, felt obliged under that statute to spell out all of the "various forms or means by which Whitman's nature was overcome and his death thereby occasioned." It goes to show how it was the murder law of the *Little Bluebook* that was probably the "Statute" meant in the indictment.

But then, maybe it was all just a hill of feathers. In most places, the *Big* and the *Little Bluebooks* drew the same bead. Lawyer Matthew Deady said the question was about as important as "which end shall an egg be broken."[49]

To the pioneer citizens on that frontier, what the written law said of murder was of no-never-mind. To them, it made no difference whether there was or was not a law library. It made no difference what the *Bluebooks* said or what the Twenty Acts would say. It made no difference that the killing took place under the Provisional Government or that the trial was taking place under the Territorial Government or that the state of law was at a crossroads between the two. The unwritten rules against murder were understood everywhere. Murder was wrong. Unfair killing must be avenged. It was that simple.

So when the indictment stated that the death of Whitman was "contrary to the form of the Statute in such case made and provided," the word "statute" was of no account to those who had ventured into wilderness. What mattered was that the killing of Whitman was contrary to the people.

Law in 1850 was plowing new furrows in the Oregon wild. People like Pratt, Holbrook, and Curry were there to make sure that those furrows were made straight and proper. But the people were there for the harvest and nothing more.

Holland finished reading the indictment, and the quiet woke people up. The indictment was signed "Amory Holbrook, U.S. Attorney for the District of Oregon." Francis Pettygrove was foreman of the grand jury, and he was there in court sitting in the jury chairs along with some of the other grand jurors. Pettygrove signed the Bill of Indictment and said it was "a true bill," meaning that the grand jurymen felt the prosecutor had enough evidence to take his case on up to this full trial.

Foreman Pettygrove was a leading citizen, a man of business. His general store was one of three in Oregon City, the others being owned by Doctor John McLoughlin of the Hudson's Bay Company, and by George Abernethy, who had been a governor of the Provisional Government. Pettygrove called his place The Red House, where he sold dried apples, sarsaparilla, molasses, ploughshares, pitchforks, cut nails, tobacco, tartan shawls, duck pants, Mackinaw blankets, and such.

Pettygrove and a lawyer by name of Asa Lovejoy were two "old Oregonians" who founded their own town downriver from Oregon City.

Lovejoy reckoned to call it Boston after his home back in Massachusetts. But Pettygrove won a coin toss and got to name it Portland after his home town in Maine. In 1848 they sold out and moved back here to Oregon City, figuring that not much was likely to come of this Portland town.[50]

That was not the only time that Pettygrove made a bad business decision. Once he bought some lumber for $1,000, then sold it to Judge Pratt for a $2,000 double profit. But Pratt got the best of it, because Pratt took the lumber down to San Francisco and sold it for $42,000.[51]

These two traders were now in court on new business: Pettygrove, as grand jury foreman, was giving Pratt, as trial judge, the power to sit in judgment on five souls charged with murder.

The next order of business called for the judge to give lawyers to the five defendants. Both *Bluebooks* said: "Sec. 64. The Court shall assign counsel to defend the prisoner, in case he cannot procure counsel himself."[52]

Could the prisoners "procure counsel" on their own? If they could not, it was not because of poverty. The tribe bred and raised some of the finest horses in the nation, known throughout the West as "Cayuses." The tribe had brought fifty head with them to Oregon City to pay trial costs. The price of a Cayuse horse was between $10 and $30. Fifty head could come to about $1,000. So it would seem the prisoners were able to procure their own counsel and none needed to be assigned. In fact, my friend Joe Meek said that the defense lawyers were paid with those horses.[53] But I have it that Joe was wrong, because Judge Pratt did assign counsel to the prisoners in accordance with the statute. Why was that? The *Bluebooks* gave a possible reason:

> Sec. 89. Offenders . . . found guilty shall be liable for all
> costs of the trial, including the fees of the witnesses on
> the part of the prosecution.[54]

Pratt must have looked ahead and seen the chance that the defendants might be found guilty. If so, they would not have money to pay for lawyers because the trial costs would use up whatever values they had. Trial costs would be high. When Leander Wallace was killed by the Snoqualmich up in Puget Sound, the trial had cost somewhere between $1,900 and $4,000, including $500 for lawyers' fees.

In this Cayuse trial, prosecutor Holbrook had summoned at least two dozen witnesses to testify before the grand jury. Those witnesses were spread all over the Territory. The costs of the marshal and his deputies in riding all over back country to serve summonses would add up. Then too, there would be prosecutor fees for writing up the indictment, pay-

Francis W. Pettygrove, ca. 1880s (?)
The grand jury foreman, Pettygrove owned a general store and traded lumber. He was also cofounder of the town of Portland, Oregon. (Courtesy Oregon Historical Society.)

ment of interpreters, fees and meals and board for jurymen, and jailing of the prisoners. Fifty horsehead would not go far in trade for those kinds of costs and would not leave much left over to procure counsel.[55] And that is why Pratt assigned counsel to the prisoners in keeping with the statute. In fact, he gave them three.

Pratt had a number of lawyers to pick from for the prisoners' counsel. To be a lawyer in those days was just a matter of setting up shop. Anyone could call himself a lawyer and give legal advice and draft legal papers. Then too, there were a lot of folks, like me, that took it as a pastime to nose about in law doings. But to appear in court and argue a case for someone was something else; that kind of lawyering was called "going beyond the bar of the court" and required court approval. In August of 1849, the first five members of the Clackamas District Bar were sworn in as officers of the court. They were "A.L. Lovejoy, A.A. Skinner, W.W. Chapman, W.T. Matlock, and David Stone."[56] And there were others around practicing law: men like Jim Nesmith, Dave Logan, and Aaron Wait. But not one of them was chosen to defend.

Chapman might have been a good choice. But he was off in Portland clearing some land, building a house, and starting up the *Oregonian* newspaper. Then too, Chapman and Pratt did not see eye to eye. Some months after the Cayuse trial, Chapman saw fit to call Pratt prejudiced. So Pratt found Chapman in contempt of court and would not let Chapman practice law before him. In return, Chapman threatened to harm the judge, so Pratt jailed him. Chapman's friends helped Chapman escape, and he stayed free until another judge released him from the contempt charge.[57] There would have to be hair on a frog before Pratt would ever allow Chapman to argue in Pratt's courtroom.

Pratt could have also picked Dave Stone. Stone was experienced. He had defended the Snoqualmich Indian murderers. Back in late September 1849, Judge William Bryant, Marshal Meek, prosecutor Skinner, defense lawyer Stone, and a bunch of jurymen rode up to Puget Sound to hold court. It was not much of a trial. No proper records were kept. But it got the job done. Two of the Snoqualmich were found guilty and hung the day after conviction.[58] Dave Stone did not win that trial, but at least he had seen the wind blow. He was not picked.

A young lawyer named Dave Logan over in the Tuality-Yamhill district was new to the Territory, but he was good with juries. He grew up around lawyers and cut his teeth on law books. His father back in Illinois was a law partner with a man named Abraham Lincoln. A year or so after this Cayuse trial, young Logan took the side of an Indian named Tom. In that case, Logan won an important argument that the defense counsel in the Cayuse trial were fixed to lose. I will have to say more about that later. But Pratt did not appoint lawyer Logan, maybe because Logan was known to pull a cork more than good sense would allow.[59]

Jim Nesmith was another lawyer who proved to be an able defender. Later on, he took the Union marshal job after Joe Meek. In 1860, Nesmith was voted senator from Oregon to the United States Congress. But he was probably not a good choice to represent the Cayuse because he had been captain in the Oregon Volunteers, a temporary militia that had gone off to run down the Cayuse in 1848 after the Whitman killing.[60]

Pratt could have chosen Aaron Wait. Wait helped start the *Spectator* newspaper, and later was the first chief judge on the Oregon Supreme Court once Oregon got statehood in 1859. In 1850 Wait was an older lawyer practicing law right here in Oregon City.[61]

For some reason, Wait and all the others did not get the job of defenders. Instead, the job went to Kintzing Pritchette, Thomas Claiborne, Jr., and Robert B. Reynolds. Pritchette was the secretary of the Territory, second in command to Governor Lane. Claiborne and Reynolds were military officers in the Mounted Rifle Regiment. Why these three were chosen is a thing to ponder.

Secretary Pritchette was a Pennsylvania lawyer and the only one of the three defenders trained in law. Marshal Meek called him "a man of brains."[62] No doubt Pritchette would lead the defense.

Pritchette's appointment put all of the Oregon Territory's top officials present at trial. They were all President Polk appointments. The governor was there spectating; the secretary was defending; the only active judge was presiding; the attorney general was prosecuting; and the marshal was keeping order. Governor Lane was pleased to have that kind of showing—a showing that brought out all of the white man's major chiefs. It was big doings, done proper and civilized.

Helping Pritchette was Tom Claiborne, a brevet captain in the Mounted Rifles. Claiborne must have been one of those platoon lawyers for the cavalry, full of legal talk but no training. He had been with the defendants since the turnover at The Dalles. As a captor, he took heart for his captives. As the trial warmed up, so did he. He knuckled to the task. Meek put it that Claiborne "foamed and ranted like he war acting a play in some theatre; he knew about as much law as one of the Indians he war defending; and his gestures were so powerful that he smashed two tumblers."[63]

Outside of the courtroom, Claiborne was also peppery and as cross as two sticks. It seems he did not like missionaries. One evening, he got into an argument with Reverend Spalding because Spalding was pestering folks around town about the trial. The *Spectator* newspaper reported that Claiborne, on "meeting Mr. Spalding on the street, addressed him in language at once severe, profane, and improper . . . and spoke of Missionaries and Clergymen generally, in exceedingly disreputable terms." Claiborne must have said something short about Marcus Whitman as well, because the *Spectator* scolded Claiborne on his "tirades of ill feeling towards the religious teachers of the country, and especially attempts to cast a shade over the memory of the dead."[64]

Claiborne's temper sometimes blinded him so much that he stumbled short of truth. He told folks that prosecutor Holbrook admitted the prisoners' innocence and that Governor Lane had promised before trial to stop any sentence of death if the judge and jury should order it. I don't see how Holbrook and Lane would say such things. Still and all, Claiborne was just headstrong, and his stretches on truth were born of vigor more than cunning. He got his rank of captain in a battlefield promotion for daring in the war down in Mexico.[65]

At trial, Claiborne was a valued helper to Pritchette. Claiborne was scribe for the defenders. It was in his hand that most of the defendants' motions, petitions, and pleas were written. He also kept the defendants' record of the trial testimony. It was a writing called the Bill of Exceptions. That made three different people keeping track of what was being said at the trial. Deputy Clerk Frank Holland kept the 1850 Order Book, the *Spectator* newspaper reporter took notes for his story, and Captain Tom Claiborne made out the defendants' Bill of Exceptions.[66]

Defense counsel Reynolds was a major and paymaster in the Mounted Rifles. Meek said he "made a very good defense." But, on whole, he was mostly quiet.[67] Both Reynolds and Claiborne were in their trooper suits. That dress might not have helped the defendants because the Mounted Rifles had been such bad citizens since coming to the Valley.

Each of these three defense counsels represented all five defendants as a group. That may not have been a good plan for some of the five. The *Bluebooks* allowed a defendant to be tried in a separate trial at the defendant's druthers.[68] At the very least, that law ought to have called for giving separate lawyers to each. As things turned out, defendant Kiamasumkin would have been helped by separate trial or separate lawyering.

The first business of the defense lawyers was to ask Judge Pratt for more time to prepare before making a plea to the indictment. Pratt figured that was fair, so he gave a thing called continuance.

Then Pratt ordered Clerk Curry to give defendants and their lawyers a copy of Indictment Number Eleven, a list of the witnesses who testified before the grand jury, and a list of the petit jury. The petit jury means the "small jury," in order to keep it separate from the grand jury, which means the "big jury." The law says that every defendant is to have two juries, one to accuse and one to make verdict. In the Cayuse indictment, the "big" jury was saying that defendants ought to be put to trial before the "small" jury. So the job of the petit jury was to decide if the defendants ought to be put to the rope. No doubt those jury names are short on horse sense, because the small jury had the biggest chore.

It would be no small order for Curry and Holland to pen copies of that long-tongued indictment. But it was what the law required. The *Blue-*

books said that in a death case, the accused should get a copy of the indictment and a list of petit jurors at least twenty-four hours before trial.[69] Pratt gave an extra twenty-four hours. So, in all, Pratt gave the defenders two days from the delivery of copies—two days to prepare to defend.

Court took leave for that morning, and the prisoners were led back to the *skookum* house.

The Afternoon of the First Day

Later that same day, at four hours past noon, court came back in session for some short business. Hardly any folks were there. The governor was gone too; he had made his showing. Defendants were not present, either.

Prosecutor Holbrook wanted the grand jury to give their "True Bills" on other indictments against these same defendants. Indictment thirteen said defendants also murdered Narcissa Whitman. Indictment Fourteen said they murdered Luke W. Saunders. Indictments Fifteen, Seventeen, Eighteen, and Nineteen said they murdered "Gillon—Christian name unknown," Jacob Hoffman, Francis Sager, and Andrew Rogers. These six other killings all happened at the same time and place as the killing of Marcus Whitman alleged in Indictment Eleven.

In fact, there were eleven people killed at Waiilatpu on November 29, 1847, and two more killed a few days later—thirteen deaths in all. Then too, Marshal Meek's daughter, Helen, died there of disease while she was held captive without doctoring. It was a heap of dying—a massacre— the *Whitman Massacre*.[70]

The indictments having been presented, the court discharged Pettygrove and the rest of the grand jury and then adjourned.

When report of the massacre reached the settlers in the Valley back in December 1847, a fire burned in their hearts as hot as the fire that burned in the Cayuse when they took to slaughter. Hot blood begets hot blood. The *Spectator* newspaper drew aim on what the blaze was like:

> [F]or the barbarian murderers . . . let them be pursued
> with unrelenting hostility, until their lifeblood has atoned
> for their infamous deeds; let them be hunted as beasts of
> prey; let their name and race be blotted from the face of
> the earth, and the places that once knew them, know
> them no more forever.[71]

The savage way in which Missus Whitman was killed was a sign of the Cayuse fire and fuel for the settlers' fire. Joe Meek was one of the first white men to reach Waiilatpu after the massacre and the captivity of the survivors. He found the murdered bodies dug from shallow graves by wolves. Missus Whitman's parts were mixed with what was left of the others. It has been said that Meek wrote this:

> It is probable Mrs. W. offered resistance, for besides the severance of the head from the body, etc., bruises exhibited themselves in many parts of her scull, which induces me to think they first struck her down with their whips, if indeed they did not finally kill her by this process.[72]

It is not likely that Joe wrote those lines. He was schooled in the Rocky Mountain College—a learning set in cold winters by a mountain campfire. There is too much letter in those lines for the likes of his learning. Joe probably told the account, and then it was set to some other writer's polish.[73]

Even so, what Joe saw when he came upon that slaughter would make blood freeze cold. Some of what he saw must have been the wolf-eaten parts of his own child. Even for a hard-living mountain trapper who had stared into the empty eyes of death many times, those remains must have been like whiskey in an open cut. I watched Joe there at trial. His outside was all marshal, but his innards had to be father.

That afternoon after the grand jurymen were discharged, I talked to one of them, a man named Sam Campbell. He said that some of his fellow jurymen blamed Catholics for the massacre. That fool notion was put there by Young Chief Tawatoe.

Tawatoe testified to the grand jury that, way back before the massacre, the Cayuse suspected that Doctor Whitman might be poisoning their sick. So the Cayuse went to a Catholic priest for advice. The priest said to them, "Make a test. Give one of your sick to Whitman for his doctoring, and give another of your sick to your *tewat* for his medicine."

So they did, said Tawatoe. As bad luck would have it, Whitman's patient died and the medicine man's patient lived, and that was fat for the fire. No doubt the priest's heart was in the right place; but as things turned out, it was a pity his advice was given and his test was used. It made it look like the massacre was Catholic doings, and that was just not so.[74]

None of Tawatoe's grand jury testimony came out at trial, but it shows something of the bad heart beating below the skin of those times—Christian differences, Protestant against Catholic.

The Morning of the Second Day

The next morning, Wednesday, May 22, 1850, at the hour of nine, Case Number Eleven, *United States v. Telokite et al.*, was back in court. Curry and Holland must have made delivery of copies of the indictment and lists, because the defenders were ready to do battle even though their two-day continuance was a long way from over. They filed a motion called a Plea in Bar. It was written by Claiborne and backed by Pritchette. Some of it said this:

> [The] Court . . . ought not to take further cognizance of the . . . Indictment . . . because . . . Defendants . . . at the time of the alleged commission . . . were native born Indians belonging to the Cayuse nation whose territory lyeth west of the summit of the Stoney or Rocky Mountains, and without the limits of the Indian Country as defined by the Congress of the United States in legislative enactments previous to the time of the alleged commission . . . and therefore not . . . subject to the jurisdiction of the Courts of the United States.

It went on and set down a second reason for no court jurisdiction:

> [D]efendants . . . further saith that Wai-il-at-pu the place where the alleged felony is supposed to have been committed, was part and parcel of the country . . . claimed and possessed by the said Cayuse nation . . . and without the jurisdiction and laws of the United States . . . and subject to the laws and usages of the said Cayuse nation . . . they being free and independent.[75]

At bottom, the Plea had the *X* marks of each of the five defendants. Judge Pratt made Claiborne take an oath that what he wrote was true and "interposed in good faith." A verification affidavit is what it was called, and "T. Claiborne" signed it.

The Plea argued that the court had no power in the case for two reasons that seemed to run contrary to one another. On one side, Claiborne was arguing that the killing happened outside of "Indian Country"; but on the other side, he was arguing that the killing happened in Cayuse country under Cayuse law and custom. The Plea spoke with a forked tongue.

Prosecutor Holbrook must have known that the Plea was coming, because he was all set with a written "Replication to Plea in Bar," which he

The United States of America
vs
Telogivoit
Tamahas
Clokomas
Isaasheluckas
Kiamasumkin

District Court of the United States of America for the District of Oregon — County of Clackamas

And the said Telogivoit, Tamahas, otherwise called Shumdmes, Clokomas, Isiaashelukas and Kiamasumkin in their own proper persons cometh into Court and having heard the Indictment read, saith that the said District Court of America, here ought not to take further cognizance of the felony in the several counts of the Indictment above specified, because protesting that they are not guilty of the felony charged in said Indictment aforesaid nevertheless the defendants Telogivoit, Tamahas, otherwise called the Shumdmes Clokomas, Isiaashelukas and Kiamasumkin say eth, that at the time [if committed] of the alleged commission of the so called felony, to wit, on the twenty ninth day of November One thousand eight hundred and forty seven, they were native born Indians belonging to the Cayuse nation, whose territory lyeth west of the summit of the Stoney or Rocky mountains, and without the limits of the Indian country as defined by the Congress of the United States in legislative enactments previous to the time of the alleged commis

---

Demurrer to the Indictment

The first page of the defendants' Plea in Bar, dated May 22, 1850, claiming that the United States courts had no jurisdiction over the Cayuse or over any crime committed west of the Rocky Mountains. (Courtesy Oregon State Archives, Clackamas County, U.S. District Court Records.)

filed with the court. The Replication sharpened the edge of difference between the prosecutor and the defenders. It said:

> [T]he offence . . . was committed . . . at a place within In-
> dian Country . . . and therefore . . . is cognizable by this
> Hon. Court.

Holbrook's indictment had alleged the same thing: the crime took place in Indian Country. But the defenders' Plea said that it did not. That quarrel was as clear as a slow creek in a mud slide. It seems like the arguments should have been just otherwise.

The reason for that turnaround was the law itself. In the law, the words "Indian Country" meant big medicine. It began back in 1834, when the United States Congress passed a law that ordered:

> [A]ll that part of the United States west of the Mississippi,
> and not within [certain states or territories . . . are]
> deemed to be the Indian country. . . .

> [S]o much of the laws of the United States as provides for
> the punishment of crimes committed within any place
> within the sole and exclusive jurisdiction of the United
> States, shall be in force in Indian Country.[76]

So Indian Country had a meaning contrary to what it seemed to say. Indian Country was not country belonging to Indians; it was country within the "sole and exclusive jurisdiction of the United States." If Wai-ilatpu was in Indian Country, then the massacre could be governed by Union law.[77]

But in 1834, when Congress passed that law, the Union border ran up to the Rocky Mountain Divide and no further. At that time, both Britain and the Union agreed that everything west of the Rockies here in the Oregon wilderness would be held by both nations and neither would have "sole and exclusive jurisdiction." So in 1834 Oregon was not Indian Country.

Then, in August 1846, the British gave up their claim to the Pacific Northwest south of Parallel Forty-nine degrees—a line that is today the Canadian border. But it was not until two years later—August 1848—that the Union jumped into the breach left by the British withdrawal. It was then that Congress brought government to the Oregon Territory. In that space of time between the Augusts of 1846 and 1848, Oregon seemed to be empty of federal government, and that is when the Whitman Massacre took place.[78]

Could the Act of 1834 be read to mean that the Union ran beyond the Rockies to the Pacific when Congress at that time had no such thought? Claiborne argued no. He said that, when the massacre happened, it happened in a place that was not yet Indian Country, not yet under the power of the Union by its own Act of 1834. The massacre was at a time and in a space of ground like between war parties, the land of no man except the Indians. Waiilatpu was Cayuse land, said Claiborne, but not Indian Country.

That stand must have been troubled footing for a cavalry officer. Horse soldiers in the West were called upon to be Indian fighters. It was their orders to push Indians back into pockets and to clear the wild for settlers. If Claiborne's heart was in his Plea in Bar, he would be hard pressed to square that with his military duty. Claiborne had been one of the officers who helped Governor Lane bring in the prisoners from The Dalles; now here he was arguing that there was no authority to do that.

But then, that is what lawyering always seems to do. One day, a lawyer will float his stick downstream; the next day, he fords against the current. It is no wonder that some believe lawyering has no soul.

But it does not matter what may have been in Claiborne's heart; what mattered was what was in Judge Pratt's mind—a political mind that had sworn allegiance to the Union and white man's laws and policy. Union policy was to give Indians "the utmost good faith . . . , justice and humanity . . . , and peace and friendship."[79] But Pratt was not about to read that policy to mean that Indians had their own pockets of government. He was not about to tell Governor Lane to release prisoners that the governor had worked so long to capture. Pratt was not about to tell President Polk that the destiny of settling Oregon was contrary to Indian jurisdiction. Pratt was not about to tell the white pioneers that their overland trip was a trespass and that there would be no trial.

The *Spectator* newspaper said that Pratt gave a "labored and very lucid opinion on the whole matter." Whether it was labored or lucid or neither or both is of no account, because, at bottom, Pratt said what every person knew he would say before the Plea was even filed. Pratt said no to the Plea in Bar and bade the case move on.[80]

That is when Pritchette jumped to his feet and said, "We take exception to the judge's ruling." The crowd sucked air in surprise. But Pritchette meant no cheek by it, and Pratt took none. It was just lawyer talk. It was necessary to "enter exception" in order that the ruling could be appealed to a higher court.

But here is a fact that would raise a smile if it were not so cruel: At the same time that the Plea in Bar was being decided in Oregon City, on the other side of the nation in Washington City, Congress was having a look at the same question. On June 5, 1850, one week after this trial ended,

Congress amended the Act of 1834 by making the Oregon Territory part of *Indian Country*.[81] Of course, there was no way that Pratt or Pritchette or Claiborne or Curry could have known that decision was in the making. There were no telegraphs in those days, and news took months to travel ocean to ocean.

Three years later, this question of jurisdiction came up again before the Oregon Territory Supreme Court, in that case I told you about against the Indian named Tom, who was defended by lawyer Logan. Tom was accused of selling liquor to Indians. Chief Judge George Williams ruled that the Oregon Territory was not part of Indian Country before June 1850:

> Oregon is generally supposed to be a part of the Indian country named in the act of Congress of June 30th, 1834; but such is not the case. . . .

> The Rocky Mountains then was the Western boundary of the United States for legislative purposes, and so continued until 1846. The act of 1834 shows in terms, that it was intended as a country over which the general government had absolute and exclusive jurisdiction. Congress by express enactment in 1850 [on June 5], extended said act to this territory, for the reason, as might be supposed, that it was not in force here before that time.[82]

Of course, the *Tom* case did not do these five defendants any good. It was water yet to fall. What is yonder and not yet reached is of no help to those who must stand in their own times.

It was time to hear the defendants plead guilty or not. With the help of the interpreters, they each said that they were innocent of the murder charged in Indictment Eleven.

Pratt ordered Curry to enter the pleas in the record and asked if there was any more business for the court.

The defenders then filed another written paper, a Petition to Change the Venue. Claiborne wrote it, and the judge made him sign it and swear it was true and made in good faith. It was also signed by the *X* marks of the defendants, but Judge Pratt did not give them oath.

The petition was read aloud, and it went down the spines of the spectators like a sharp stick.

> "[Petitioners] cannot have a fair and impartial trial . . . within the County of Clackamas . . . because . . . many

they will be put to death.

To sum up your Petitioners fully believe that
the inhabitants of the County are so prejudiced
against them, that they cannot expect an impartial
trial

And, that, the prosecution has an undue influence
over the minds of the inhabitants of the County.
and therefore they pray your honor to
have this case removed, to be tried in Clark
County, adjoining that an impartial
trial may be had

Telaquoit   his + mark
Tamahas   his + mark
Clokomas   his + mark
Isiaasheluckas   his + mark
Kiamasumkin   his + mark

Personally came into Court the above named
Petitioners Telaquoit, Tamahas, Clokomas,
Isiaasheluckas and Kiamasumkin and
made oath that to the best of their knowledge
the facts contained in the above petition are
true

Telaquoit   his mark
Tamahas   his mark
Clokomas   his mark
Isiaasheluckas his mark
Kiamasumkin   his mark

Petition to Change the Venue

The last page of the defendants' motion to seek removal of the trial to Clark
County (north of the Columbia River) because of prejudice and vindictiveness on
the part of the inhabitants of Oregon City. (Courtesy Oregon State Archives,
Clackamas County, U.S. District Court Records.)

> among the most respectable citizens of said County have used threats of death toward your petitioners in case of acquittal, and further because the most respectable and influential citizens in said County . . . have used . . . their powerful influence to influence the public mind against your petitioners, and because furthermore it is daily asserted . . . [by] many [of] the most influential citizens that your petitioners shall suffer death, whether or not they are acquitted. . . . [S]o great is the general desire . . . of the people of Clackamas to avenge themselves, that your petitioners have no hope of a fair trial . . . [and] fully believe that they will be put to death.

> [T]he inhabitants of the County are so prejudiced . . . that [petitioners] cannot expect an impartial trial.

> [T]he prosecution has an undue influence over the minds of the inhabitants . . . , and therefore [petitioners] pray your honor to have this case removed to be tried in Clark County, adjoining."

Pratt had to hammer for order. The words of that petition put the citizens in their chins and down at their corners. It said they were unfair people, prejudiced people, vengeful people.

Whether it was fair to say that of them was each man's notion. But one thing was dead certain: most of the settlers in the Valley knew of the Whitmans. Missus Narcissa Whitman was one of the first two white women to come overland to Oregon Country. The older mountain men and Hudson's Bay trappers had shared the early wilderness with the Whitmans. The new settlers carried loving memory of the charity given at the Whitman sanctuary way back on that godforsaken trail to the Valley. It was a kindness of which deep heart is made.

Take for a sample this: Sitting in the courtroom next to me was a man in his young twenties named Anson Cone. He and I had talked while we were waiting for the trial to start. He told me about his coming overland in 1846 and stopping at Waiilatpu when he was nineteen years of age. Whitman gave him provender and an old white Cayuse pack horse named Bob. Cone was mighty obliged and said that Whitman "was a good man—a heart like an ox." As luck was to have it, young Cone at this trial ended up serving on the jury to decide who were Whitman's murderers.[83]

The reporter for the *Spectator* newspaper saw the citizens at Oregon City different than the defenders saw them:

The circumstances attending this trial reflect the highest degree of credit on the people of this Territory. It is scarcely possible that more intense feeling could possess every bosum than has prevailed here in regard to this trial. And yet it all passed off with the most perfect quiet. From two hundred to three hundred persons were present during the trial but never in a single instance did we witness the slightest impropriety of conduct. The solemnity and stillness of a church characterized the court room during the whole proceeding.[84]

Then too, Reverend George H. Atkinson, another Protestant minister who was there, wrote down in his diary: "The court room exhibited a scene of perfect order and propriety, no rush, no crowding. . . . [T]hey looked feelingly upon the adjudged."[85]

But back east in reports of this trial, some said of Oregon City that it was a "nasty town," an "accursed town," and said of the settlers that they were "sunk in oblivion that is the fate of those who are born without souls."[86]

Yet when all is said and done, the opinion that counts most in a courtroom is the opinion of the judge, and Judge Pratt could see no "public excitement" afoot. He overruled Claiborne and said the case was not to be tried anywhere but right here in Oregon City.

This time, Pritchette took no exception to the judge's ruling. It was not easy for the secretary of the Territory to approve of charges made against the very citizenry he represented. He must have felt that the venue change was a shot too long and just a flash in Claiborne's pan.

It seems to me that Claiborne had the right bead, but he just loaded wrong. He argued that hot blood in Oregon City was the reason for a different trial place. He should have argued that it was the *lay of the land*, not the *airs*, that was wrong for trial. He should have argued that Waiilatpu, the place of the murder, was outside the bounds of the Clackamas court district.

Back in September, Oregon lawmakers had cut the Territory into three judicial districts, just as Congress directed in the Territorial Act.[87] The first district, called "Clackamas County" in the petition, was all of the territory east of the Willamette River and south of both the Columbia River and a line drawn on Parallel Forty-six degrees.[88] The second district was west of the Willamette and does not matter here. The third district, called "Clark County" in the petition, was all of the territory north of the Columbia and north of Parallel Forty-six degrees. If aim is taken on Parallel Forty-six, it can be seen that it lies south of Waiilatpu about five or ten miles. So the massacre happened north of the Clackamas border and should have been venued in the third district, Clark County, where Claiborne wanted it.

But the defense lawyers cannot be blamed. Few people in those years knew where Parallel Forty-six was or why it had even been chosen. The Snake River bend would have been a more natural border. There were no maps showing the parallel, and the surveyors had not yet begun staking their lines. The Cayuse defendants were of no help, either. Indians were the last people on earth to understand what a *shuyapu* land boundary was. In those days, land claims and boundaries were fixed to run along lines of nature, like from a ridge or the bottom of a draw or some tree stump. Great trust was placed in banks of rivers. That was how Parallel Forty-six might have been muzzle-sighted. It ran on a line in rough keeping with the Walla Walla River. Waiilatpu was on the north bank of the Walla Walla. So that put the killing of Whitman in the third district, and the case would have been tried there if folks would have known.[89]

In May 1850, these venue lines put things in a mighty curious situation. Presidents Polk and Taylor never got around to picking a judge for the third district. Judge Bryant of the first district in Oregon City was gone from Oregon. That meant the lawmakers had to call Judge Pratt over from Lafayette in the second district to run things in Oregon City. So the situation came down to this: A second-district judge sat in the first district on a murder that happened in the third district. All of civilization's tidy ends had to be loosened in order to tie up the more important business of getting the job done. But the lawyers made no quarrel on that point, and that meant the defendants had no right to complain later on. So it was settled that the trial was to be held here and now.

Prosecutor Holbrook then brought out two of the other indictments filed yesterday: Indictment Thirteen for the killing of Missus Whitman and Indictment Fourteen for the killing of Luke Saunders. These were all part of the massacre. His Honor said it was time for "arraignment" on those two killings.

The defending lawyers said it was not necessary to read aloud those indictments. Everyone breathed relief at that. The defending lawyers said that they did not need to receive copies either. Deputy Holland breathed relief at that.

The lawyers asked Pratt for more time to plead to the Missus Whitman and Luke Saunders indictments. Pratt said yes to that. So those indictments were laid aside and nothing more ever came of them. Neither did Holbrook bring out the indictments for the killings of "Gillon," Jake Hoffman, Frank Sager, or Andy Rogers. The Cayuse were going to be tried under Indictment Eleven for the killing of Marcus Whitman and for no other.[90] It was to be a single-murder trial, not a massacre trial. That was an aim that ought to have been kept straight, but as the trial moved on it went far from the mark.

Another thing that was hard to keep straight was the names and faces of the defendants. The indictment on Missus Whitman's killing had a sixth defendant named Isholhol. That was likely just another name for defendant Isiaasheluckas. So Holbrook had named that defendant twice.

Then too, Indictment Sixteen was called "United States versus Frank Escaloom." But Escaloom was likely still another name for Isiaasheluckas.

It was all just a problem of white folks trying to put Indian tongue into written King's English and of missionaries baptizing Indians under Christian names. Chief Telokite's son had his Cayuse name spelled Shumahici; that was translated "Painted Shirt," and yet he was baptized Frank. So he was called three different ways. And you can add a fourth: in Chinook Jargon he would be called *Pent Shut*.

Defendant Chief Telokite's name was spelled many different ways in the trial record: Telokite, Telakite, Tilikite, Teloquoit, and whatever else.[91] That kind of whatchamacallhim was all a part of a bigger problem. In a face, white folks saw "Injun" only, and Indians saw *shuyapu* only, and no one saw heart.

Pratt ordered adjournment until next morning at the hour of nine.

The Morning of the Third Day

At nine o'clock on the forenoon of Thursday, May 23, 1850, everyone came together for the third trial day. It was to be a long one. The crowd was there in full, for they reckoned that the law talk was all done and that the court was set to hear witnesses tell the facts. Folks yearned to hear what happened at the massacre and during the captivity. Most of what was known was just gossip and yarns that were two parts notion mixed to only one part fact. It was a story so ugly not even the newspaper would tell of it. The *Spectator* put it this way:

> In our career as public journalist . . . we have never shrunk from our duty, in recording events howsoever painful and abhorrent to our feelings, but in this case our pen refuses—we dare not chronicle the terrible story of their wrongs.[92]

A report like that was just the smell of biscuits and gravy. So, on this day, after two and one half years, starved bellies had come to the trough.

But there was still more lawyer doings to keep them from feed. Deputy Holland got up and read from the Order Book the minutes of yesterday's

Chief Telokite, ca. 1847
One of the five accused and the leader of the Waiilatpu band of the Cayuse.
This watercolor is one of several differing likenesses of Telokite by Paul Kane.
(Courtesy Stark Museum of Art, Orange, Texas.)

court business. Judge Pratt approved and signed the book: "O.C. Pratt—Judge 2d Jud. Dis. Oregon Territory."

After that, the Cayuse lawyers argued for "continuance of the cause," meaning they wanted more time to get ready. They filed an affidavit of Chief Telokite, saying defendants needed to have a witness by the name of Quishem summoned.[93] Quishem was two hundred fifty miles back east in Cayuse country. If Governor Lane had been in court, he would have dropped fat in the fire. Lane had come a long way to bring five Cayuse in from their country, and for certain he was not about to turn back to bring in another.

So that request had about as much chance as a prairie dog in a wolf's mouth. Pratt would have none of it.

But even though it was denied, Telokite's affidavit gave a clue as to how the Cayuse lawyers fixed to defend:

> Telokite . . . makes oath that . . . Quishem now in Cayuse country, he thinks will be a material witness. . . . That the materiality of . . . [Quishem] was not known in time to have him in attendance at this time. . . . [S]aid witness will prove that the late Dr. Whitman administered medicines to many of the Cayuse Indians and that afterwards a large number of them died, including the wives and children of some of these defendants. . . . [A] certain Joseph Lewis . . . informed these defendants a few days before the 29 November 1847 that the Cayuse Indians were dying in consequence of poison being administered to them by the late Marcus Whitman and [Telokite] had heard Dr. Whitman say that he would kill off all of the Cayuse Indians by the coming of the ensuing Spring— that he would then have their horses and lands. Witness will also prove that it is the law of the Cayuse Indians to kill bad medicine men.

It takes no extra brains to see that that affidavit was not in the words of Chief Telokite. The script looked to be from the hand of Claiborne. He was probably penning Telokite's thoughts.[94] But even though it began by saying that Telokite "makes oath," no written oath appeared on it, and Telokite did not give it his mark.

Judge Pratt ruled the affidavit was "insufficient." But if it was insufficient because of no oath or signing, that would have been a simple matter to cure in court. Maybe no swearing was given because Pratt saw a religious problem in Indian oath-taking. Still, that would not seem enough to make Telokite's affidavit insufficient, because later an Indian named Stickus was allowed to testify at trial without oath. It was all mighty curious.

Whether sufficient or not and whether the words of Telokite or Claiborne, the affidavit gave a clue to how Telokite would defend. In so many words, it confessed the killing but said the killing was fitting and proper.

Next, Judge Pratt told Marshal Joe Meek to get the jury into the courtroom. Joe went to the door and called out, and the jury filed in—twenty-four men that Meek had ready just as the *Bluebooks* said to do. They were kept out of court because it would have tainted them to hear the lawyer doings of the last two days. Some were in their best collar and store coat, but most wore field clothes. I knew the faces of some. Joe Parrot was there. He lived upriver from The Falls at a place where a creek comes into the Willamette just before it turns to head west. The creek is named after him—Parrot Creek. Later on, a little town sprung up there called New Era. Parrot had been busy hewing timbers to build the first courthouse, but he had to put down his adz when Meek hauled him in to serve jury duty.

Albion Post was also among the twenty-four. Albion was a harness maker who set shop in Oregon City. I knew all of their faces except one. He was a stranger, and I have never seen him since. It could be that he was not qualified to be a juryman, but I cannot say that for a fact. Jurors had to be qualified to vote. That left out womenfolk and boys under age twenty-one. There was no such thing as jurywomen. Then too, law said jurymen were not allowed to be gospel ministers, doctors, or men over age sixty.[95]

It was not easy in those days to get jurymen to serve. For a good many years, folks had been on their own and away from the bit and harness of law. It took a lot of tugging to get them back into citizenship duties like voting and taxpaying. For jury call, a body would have to leave his farming and come a far distance. Many would not do it. Marshal Meek would have to go out and drag them in. It meant a lot of travel, even for an old mountain trapper like Joe who had seen more lonely miles than any hundred men put together.

One time a man named Charley Brown got out of jury duty by telling the judge, "Whar I cum from back in Missouri, they 'lowed I hadn't sense enuff to be a juryman." His argument had some teeth, because the *Bluebooks* said that "all persons not of sound mind" were not for jury call.[96]

The twenty-four men that Meek brought in were not the jury yet. They had been called thirty days in advance in keeping with the *Bluebooks*. Judge Pratt called them "a panel." Clerk Curry reached into a sack and pulled out twelve of their names on twelve slips of paper. He told those twelve to go up and have seats in the jury chairs.[97]

Prosecutor Holbrook asked each of the twelve if he grinded his axe against missionaries. Then Holbrook wanted to know if any of them felt conscience about hanging murderers. Holbrook's questioning was short.

But the Cayuse lawyers fired many questions. They wanted to know if the jurymen had heard much about the massacre and if they had any fixed notions about it. They also wanted to know what the jurymen thought of Indians.

The answers to all of that questioning were much the same from all of the jurymen: A man who murdered deserved to hang; missionaries were doing God's work; the massacre was common knowledge; an Indian was God's creature and free to go his own way so long as that way did not savage whites.[98]

Some of the jurymen were thrown out. Each time that happened, a new one of the twenty-four took his place. By and by, the lawyers went through all twenty-four jurymen, and there were still some empty seats in the jury box with no more to pick. Pratt solved that problem by telling Meek to rope in men from the crowd.

The bystanders picked did not much cotton to that. Young Anson Cone, who was sitting next to me, turned to the man on his other side and said, "Come, let's go; they will be getting us on the jury." The two of them promptly left; but in short time they were brought back under the grab of one of Meek's deputies. And so young Mister Cone was put in the jury box. After some questions and answers, he was allowed to serve even though, as I said before, he knew the victim Whitman and was obliged to Whitman because Whitman gave him horse, provender, and kindness back on the overland trail.[99]

After a time, the jury box was filled with "twelve good and lawful men of the County" to the liking of both sides. The Cayuse lawyers cut loose twenty from the herd and Holbrook cut two. "Peremptory challenge" was the lawyer name for it.[100]

The jury was now "impanelled," as Judge Pratt called it. Their names were Hiram Straight, Joseph Parrot, J.T. Hunsaker, William A. Cason, Andrew Jackson, Albion Post, Samuel Welch, Joseph Olfrey, John Densmore, Anson Cone, John Ellenburgh, and A.B. Holcomb.[101] Judge Pratt made the twelve of them stand and put a hand to heaven:

> "You solemnly swear that without respect to person, or favor, or fear, you will well and truly try and true deliverance make between the United States of America and the prisoners at bar, whom you shall have in charge, according to the evidence given you in court, and the laws of this Territory, so help you God."[102]

Anson S. Cone, ca. 1890s (?)

A petit juror who was conscripted to serve from the crowd of spectators at trial. (Courtesy Oregon Historical Society.)

The jurymen all nodded and said yea, but I suspect that few of them got the drift of those words all piled in on one another.

Prosecutor Holbrook then made a speech to the jurymen about what was charged in the indictment. Many of them had not been allowed in court and had not heard the indictment read two days ago. But those that Meek had roped in from the crowd had already heard plenty, including the petition to change venue. In that petition, the defenders called Clackamas citizens vengeful and prejudiced and such. That was a swallow still in the throat and might not have gone down well for the prisoners.

When Holbrook finished his "brief review of matters in the indictment," he called his first witness, Missus Eliza Hall. Folks sat up. Doings were finally getting to what happened two and a half years and two and a half hundred miles yonder in the ryegrass of eastern Oregon.

Missus Hall looked to be thirty or thirty-five years of age. It was hard to tell the years of a frontier woman. Pioneering made its mark on face and hands. She begat five youngsters over a ten-year period. But I'll say no more of it, because it is not civil to talk of a woman's child-bearing.

She put her hand on the Bible, and Judge Pratt gave her the oath: "Missus Hall, you do swear upon the Holy Evangelists of Almighty God to tell the truth?"[103] She said yea, took a seat, and then commenced to answer Holbrook's questions. But the questioning did not get far. Judge Pratt said that it was lunchtime. So once more the spectators were led to trough and then turned away. Pratt told Meek to take charge of the jury and keep them together. He told the jury not to talk to or listen to anybody about the case. Then he told everyone to be back in court by half past the hour of two o'clock. It had been a long morning.

The five Cayuse prisoners must have been wondering what to make of it all. Nobody had yet smoked a pipe. It had all been strange *wawa* — indictments, pleas in bar, changes of venue, motions for continuance, challenges of jurymen, and such. *Shuyapu* lawyering had been going on like that for two suns and half another.

The interpreters were having a time of it as well. At first the translations were a steady murmur beneath what was being said aloud in English. But by and by, the interpreters shook their heads and quit, mostly. Like the wrong ford of a river, the law words were too fast, too deep, too mud-bottomed.

Chief Telokite in shackles and Young Chief Tawatoe in the crowd sat stone-faced. They could understand some of the *shuyapu* words. But even if they could have understood it all, they could not have understood laws for fair doings. Fair doings came from good heart, not from laws; and Telokite scorned the *shuyapu* heart. Joe Meek told me that Telokite told his captors, "What sort of heart have you that you offer food to me, whose hands are red with your brother's blood?"[104]

The Afternoon of the Third Day

I made it to be the hour of two o'clock when court started up again that afternoon. Deputy Holland called it the same; he wrote down "2 o'clock" in the Order Book. This was one half hour before Pratt said he would start when he took leave for lunch. Pratt seemed to be in a hurry now. He wanted to get all the testimony in before the end of the day.

Then again, Pratt's early start might have been just the difference in timepieces. In those days clocks ran close but not the same. There was no Western Union or railroad to keep every man's pocket clock on the same rails. Those that had a timepiece took it proud, and each would argue that his time was best. So when Pratt said half past two and Deputy Holland marked down two in the Order Book, that might have been just the difference in their clock hands. It did not matter much except to those spectators who came late and had to miss out some.

When it came to the matter of time, Indians had a different measure. Indian time and white man's time were as different as a hawk and a handsaw. Where a white man talked of years, the Indian would say "snows." Indians spoke of "moons," not months; "suns," not days. To an Indian, the trial for this afternoon started somewhere between "high sun" and "sundown." As for minutes, there an Indian did not care a lick. Coming late and missing out or coming early and waiting was of no bother to the first Americans.

The witness, Missus Eliza Hall, seated herself in the witness chair and made ready to get on with her testimony. Judge Pratt told her to remove her bonnet because it was important that the jury should not just hear her voice but should see her face as well.

I will tell you as best as I recollect the questions put and answers given by the witnesses. But there is no word-for-word record of that. My memory follows what was set down in the *Spectator* newspaper article and the Bill of Exceptions kept by Claiborne.[105]

Prosecutor Holbrook asked the questions:

Q: Now go back, Missus Hall, to November 29, 1847. Were you present at Waiilatpu, the mission of Doctor Marcus Whitman?

A: Yes. We were living at the Mansion House. We had been there about three months.

Q: Were members of your family there?

A: Yes. My husband, Peter, and five children. My husband drowned trying to escape the Cayuse.

Q: What is the Mansion House?

A: It was the emigrant house, one of the buildings at the mission. There was the Mansion where several families stayed, the Mission House where Doctor Whitman and his wife lived with their orphans, a sawmill, a blacksmith shop, and an Indian lodge.[106]

Q: What happened that day, November 29? What did you first see and hear?

A: I heard gunshots.

Q: Where were you then?

A: At the Mansion House—inside.

Q: So you heard gunshots. Then what happened?

A: I heard the shots—many of them. I went to the door of the Mansion House and saw Telokite striking the Doctor with a hatchet.

Q: Who is "the Doctor"?

A: Doctor Whitman.

Q: The victim in this murder trial—Marcus Whitman?

A: Yes.

Q: You saw Telokite striking him. Where was this?

A: In the face. The Doctor was on the ground, and Telokite was hitting him with the hatchet in the face.

Q: I mean, where were they?

A: Outside the Mission House, about six feet from the kitchen.

Q: How many times did Telokite strike Doctor Whitman?

A: Three times.

Q: Is Telokite one of the defendants in this case?

A: Yes. There. [*Pointing to one of the accused.*][107]

Q: Did you see anyone else being assaulted?

A: Yes. The Indians were fighting Hoffman—I don't know his first name.

Q: What became of him?

A: I don't know. The last I saw he had fallen.

Q: So what did you do then?

A: I went to the Mission House.

Q: You were at the Mansion House, and you went to the Mission House? I get those mixed.

The Whitman Mission (Waiilatpu)

This view of the murder site looks southward and purportedly depicts the mission as of 1843. The T-shaped Mission House (the Whitmans' residence) is on the right and the Mansion House (immigrants' lodgings) on the lower left, with the blacksmith's shop in between. The gristmill is at the upper left. A branch of the Oregon Trail is in the foreground. The mill pond is at the left, and its irrigation ditch in the background runs toward a confluence with the Walla Walla River in the woods beyond. Today the grounds (near Walla Walla, Washington) are maintained by the National Park Service as a national historic site, open to the public. Sketch by H.D. Nichols (courtesy Oregon Historical Society).

A: That's right. I went inside the Mission House, where I found Doctor Whitman sitting on the sofa. He was wounded in several places.

Q: Was anyone else there?

A: Yes. Missus Whitman. She asked me to help take the Doctor to another room, which I did.

Q: Did Doctor Whitman die?

A: Yes. He died that night at nine o'clock.

Q: At the time you helped Missus Whitman carry the Doctor to another room, did anything happen to her?

A: She was shot, too. By the Indians. I put her wounded body on a settee in the Mission House. That's when Tomsucky came in and told me I had to go home—back to the Mansion House.

Q: And did you go?

A: I surely did.

Q: Is this Tomsucky one of the defendants here?

A: No, he is not.[108]

Q: Was anyone else assaulted by the Indians at that time?

A: When I was on my way back to the Mansion House, I heard the report of guns behind me. I turned and saw Mister Rogers throw up his hands.[109]

Then Holbrook leaned away and said he had no more questions. So the Cayuse lawyers asked the widow some.[110]

Q: Missus Hall, how far apart were the Mission House and the Mansion House?

A: I guess about a hundred yards.

Q: So when you say you saw Telokite striking Whitman, you were a hundred yards away?

A: Yes.

Q: Were there obstructions in your way—trees, buildings, anything?

A: Other Indians, maybe.

Q: Your view was obstructed, then?

A: There were several Indians standing between me and Telokite.

Q: So there were other Indians between you and what you saw over one hundred yards away?

A: Yes.[111]

Q: When you saw Mister Rogers "throw up his hands," how far were you from him?

A: About thirty yards.

Q: Your testimony then is that you saw Telokite striking Whitman, but you did not recognize any other Indians doing so?

A: Yes.

Q: Did you see other Indians there that day?

A: Yes.

Q: But they were not armed, were they?

A: Some were, but the greater portion were not.

Q: In those days at Waiilatpu, the Cayuse were sick with disease, were they not?

A: Yes, measles prevailed.

Q: And many of them died?

A: Yes.

Q: Did Whitman treat them?

A: The Doctor was a physician. He administered medicines to them.

The Cayuse lawyers had no more questions for Widow Hall, so Judge Pratt told her to leave the witness chair. She moved into the crowd and took the hand of her five-year-old daughter, Rebecca. Juryman Anson Cone did not know then that he was watching his future sister-in-law. Down the road a ways, Anson's brother, Philander, and little Miss Rebecca were to be married.[112] It goes to show how small an outpost of souls gets to be in a land big for loneliness.

Then Holbrook called his second witness, Miss Elizabeth Sager. She wore her hair combed long with a ribbon and no bonnet, as was the manner of children in those times. Missus Robb had her dressed out in gingham. Miss Elizabeth was old for her twelve years. She already had lost two fathers, two mothers, and two brothers. Her real folks both died on the immigrant trail coming overland in 1844. She and her two brothers and four sisters were taken up by the Whitmans as orphans. The Whitmans came to be father and mother to those young ones. The massacre took her second parents and her two brothers as well. Since the massacre, she had been separated from her sisters and orphaned from family to family here in the Valley. She had first been put with Missus Howland, then Missus Johnson, then Reverend Parrish, and now she was with the Robb family. In the years after the trial, she was quartered at two other homes before striking out on her own as a schoolteacher.[113] Miss Elizabeth was a child, but she had been down more roads than those who live life full.

Judge Pratt took time explaining to her the oath to be truthful. Then Holbrook started on his questions.

Massacre Survivors, ca. 1890s

The four prosecution witnesses are either present or represented in this group photograph. Elizabeth Sager Helm (*seated left*) and Lorinda Bewley Chapman (*seated center*) testified at the trial, as did Eliza Hall, the mother of Gertrude Denny (*seated right*), and Josiah Osborne, the father of Nancy Jacobs (*standing center*). (Courtesy Oregon Historical Society.)

Q: Elizabeth, before you came to this valley, where did you live?

A: Waiilatpu.

Q: Doctor Marcus Whitman's mission?

A: Yes.

Q: How long did you live there?

A: Maybe four years.

Q: Were you living there when Doctor Whitman died?

A: Yes.

Q: What date was that when he died?

A: I don't remember.

Q: Was it November 29, 1847?

A: I don't know.

Q: What happened on the day he died?

A: An Indian came to the door and asked for Father.[114]

Q: And "Father" is?

A: Doctor Whitman.

Q: Then what happened?

A: I heard loud talk and guns shooting.

Q: Did you see the shooting?

A: I saw Indians pointing guns.

Q: Who or what were they shooting?

A: I didn't see.

Q: Did they shoot Doctor Whitman?

A: I didn't see that, but I saw he was wounded. I saw Mother and Missus Hall dressing his wounds.

Q: Then what happened?

A: Mother was shot.

Q: You mean Missus Narcissa Whitman?

A: Yes.

Q: Was she killed?

A: Not then. Just bleeding.

Q: Was Doctor Whitman killed?

A: Next morning I saw him dead.

Q: Did you see anybody else hurt by the Indians?

A: Yes. Isiaasheluckas and Tomsucky were trying to throw down Mister Saunders, our schoolteacher. They shot him. He fell down, and next morning he was found dead there.

Q: Do you see those two Indians here?

A: That's Isiaasheluckas there [*pointing*], but Tomsucky is not here.

Q: Was anybody else hurt?

A: My brother was killed.[115]

Q: Besides Isiaasheluckas, were any of these other prisoners there during the killings?

A: Next day, Clokomas—that one [*pointing*]—was sitting in the Mission House. He was laughing and talking a lot. He pointed a gun at my sister.

Holbrook then told the Cayuse lawyers that they could ask their questions of Miss Elizabeth.

Q: Now, Elizabeth, when Clokomas pointed the gun at your sister, was he being serious or just jocose, er, just laughing?

A: I think he was just trying to frighten her—making fun.

Q: Now, you didn't see who shot Doctor Whitman, did you?

A: No.

Q: And you were only ten years old when all of this happened?

A: Yes.

Q: In those days at the mission was there disease among the Indians?

A: Yes, a lot were dead and dying. Five or six died sick every day.

Q: Did Doctor Whitman give them medicine for their sickness?

A: Oh, yes.

Q: Was there a man named Joe Lewis at the mission in those days?

A: Yes.

Q: And he was there on the day of Doctor Whitman's death?

A: Yes.

Q: On the evening before the Doctor's death, did Joe Lewis tell you something about what he was going to do?

A: Yes. Joe told me he was going to tell the Indians to kill him.

Q: "Him?" To kill whom?

A: To kill him — Joe Lewis.

Q: You mean Doctor Whitman, don't you? Joe Lewis said he would tell the Indians to kill Whitman; is that right?

A: [*No reply*][116]

Q: And did you believe him?

A: Not then, I didn't.

The child Elizabeth had no more to tell.[117] His Honor told her to step away. Prosecutor Holbrook then called his third witness, Missus Lorinda Chapman. When this young lady came out of the crowd she turned some heads and set up a whisper. She was in her young twenties and cut a good figure—sunshine hair and blue eyes. Story and yarning had it that she was abused by the Cayuse during the captivity of survivors that followed the massacre. Some say that she was "violated" by Chief Five Crows and others. All such talk was at corners and in hush, because it was not seemly to a woman's honor to speak of such indecency. Judge Pratt was certainly not going to allow it in this trial.

Missus Chapman's name was Miss Bewley during the massacre. She wed a man named William Chapman ten months after the massacre and twenty months before the trial. Her calico dress made a swish as she went to the witness chair. Her bonnet was held in two tight hands.[118] She swore to the truth, and Holbrook commenced to ask.

Q: Mrs. Chapman, going back to November 29, 1847, where were you?

A: I was at the mission of Doctor Whitman in Oregon.

It was Judge Pratt who wrote into the record those last five words, "of Doctor Whitman in Oregon." The records being kept by Claiborne and the newspaperman did not report those words. But His Honor recollected and saw fit to change Claiborne's Bill of Exceptions to make it state that the witness so testified. There was an important reason for those five words, and I will explain why later on.[119]

Q: You say you were at the mission; where exactly?

A: In the Mission House—upstairs—in bed. I was sick.

Q: While you were there, what happened?

A: I heard loud and angry talk down in the kitchen.

Q: What time was this?

A: Afternoon. About half past one o'clock.[120]

Q: Did you recognize the voices?

A: It was the voice of Telokite.

Q: Are you certain it was his voice?

A: Yes. I heard it distinctly. I knew his voice from hearing him rehearse for Doctor Whitman.

Q: "Rehearse"? I don't understand.

A: I could not understand one word that Telokite spoke. He was speaking in Cayuse. But I recognized his voice because he was the Doctor's interpreter, and I had heard him rehearse for Doctor Whitman before.[121]

Q: Did you see Telokite?

A: Not that day, no.

Q: You heard this loud, angry talking in the kitchen. Then what?

A: Then there were gunshots and confusion.

Q: So what did you do?

A: I got out of bed and came downstairs.

Q: What did you see there?

A: People were bringing the Doctor in from the kitchen. He was wounded. There was a cut across his face.

Q: Was he dead?

A: No. He was alive but wounded when last I saw him before I left the Mission House.

Right there, it seemed to me, the prosecutor's witnesses were knocking horns. Witness Hall had said that she saw Whitman struck down outdoors. But now here, Witness Chapman was saying that she heard Whitman being struck down in the kitchen.

Q: Did you ever see him dead?

A: The next morning I saw the Indians rolling his dead body about.

Q: You say you left the Mission House. When was that?

A: I started in the company of Mister Rogers and Missus Whitman to go to the Mansion House. Joe Lewis was helping carry Missus Whitman into the yard. When we got to the kitchen door, Mister Rogers and Missus Whitman were killed.

Q: What did you do?

A: I could not stir with alarm.[122]

Q: While standing there, did you see any of the five prisoners at bar?

A: Yes. All of them were there except Telokite. I recognize the faces of all of them. All four were present there that day. I recollect them distinctly. I also saw Tomsucky and Joe Lewis and the sons of Telokite.

Q: Were there any other killings?

A: Yes. Two persons were killed by the Indians[123] a week later while we were in captivity.

Holbrook then said he had no more to ask. The Cayuse lawyers put their questions to Missus Chapman. They asked about the sickness in the tribe and about how Doctor Whitman gave medicine for it. They also laid stress on how she only heard and never saw Telokite.

Holbrook called his fourth and last witness, Josiah Osborne. Osborne had been through a lot. He was one of the few men who made it through the massacre. The massacre victims were all men save for Missus Whitman. Osborne escaped with his missus and three young ones. The escape was rough doings, and his young son died on account of it. But that is a different story and one that was not told at trial.[124] Osborne's memory and jaw were set hard by those times.

Sawdust stuck to the drilling of his britches and mud to the kipskin of his Sunday boots. He hung tight to his galluses until Pratt made him swear upon the "Holy Evangelists of Almighty God" to tell the truth. Then came Holbrook's questions:

Q: On November 29, 1847, where were you, Mister Osborne?

A: Waiilatpu, much to my regret.

Q: That'd be *Doctor Whitman's Mission*?[125]

A: Correct.

Q: And your family was with you?

A: Yes.

Q: At the time of the incident involved in this case, where were you?

A: In Doctor Whitman's house—the Mission House. I was sick.[126]

Q: When did you first become aware of what was happening?

A: I heard the discharge and report of guns. So I went to the door and looked out. I saw Mister Kimble running by. He was wounded. I closed the door immediately and went to the window. I saw Tomahas pursuing Mister Saunders. He stopped Saunders from going towards his family. Tomahas was armed. Joe Lewis was there, too.

Q: Do you recognize either of those men in this courtroom—Tomahas or Lewis?

A: Lewis ain't here. But that's Tomahas there. [*Pointing to one of the defendants.*]

Q: Is Tomahas the one who is also called "The Murderer"?

A: Yes.

That last question is not in Claiborne's Bill of Exceptions or the *Spectator* newspaper story. But I recollect it being asked by Holbrook almost every time the name of Tomahas came up.[127]

Q: So what did you do then?

A: I got my family and we secreted ourselves under the floor.

Q: How high was the *door* of the *Mansion* House?

Tomahas, ca. 1847

One of the five accused Cayuse. Tomahas was nicknamed "The Murderer" by his own tribe long before the massacre. Painting by Paul Kane (courtesy Royal Ontario Museum, Toronto).

A: Three feet high from the ground.

That was a curious question for Holbrook to ask. It made no sense to ask how high the *Mansion* House *door* was. But that was the way the *Spectator* newspaperman reported it. Claiborne did not even bother to put it down in the Bill of Exceptions. And I have no memory of it, either. It was a question that showed how tired Holbrook, the newspaperman, and all of us were getting as the day wore down. What Holbrook asked or meant to ask was, "How high was the *floor* of the *Mission* House?" because that was where Osborne hid his wife and young ones.[128]

Q: While you were under the floor were you able to tell what was going on?

A: I heard murder going on.

Q: Can you be more specific, Mister Osborne?

A: I heard the Indians kill Missus Whitman, Mister Rogers, and a young man.[129]

Q: One more question: Do you know the nationality and race of Doctor Whitman?

A: Yes. He was a white American citizen.

What difference should it make if Whitman was a foreigner or an Indian or a white American citizen? Murder is murder all the same. The only question that should have mattered was: Was Marcus Whitman a human being? But race and nationality must have been important to Prosecutor Holbrook, because he not only asked Osborne about it, he put it in the indictment at three different places. Nowhere in the murder laws was it written that the victim had to be a white American. But even so, only a fool would deny what travels in the heart unwritten. When an Indian killed another Indian or a foreigner or when a white man killed an Indian, that sparked at tinder more wet than when an Indian killed a white American. Holbrook was a sort who would fan such coals, even if the law did not.[130]

Holbrook sat himself down. So then the Cayuse lawyers took a turn at Osborne.

Q: Were there always a lot of Indians around the mission?

A: Sometimes. They would come over for certain events.

Q: Events like the killing of a beef?

A: Yes.

Q: And were the Whitmans slaughtering a beef that day?

A: Yes.

Q: So there were Indians assembled there that day for that reason, weren't there?

A: Yes.

The defender lawyers asked those questions just to show that some Cayuse were at the mission that day for a reason other than massacre. Just because there were Cayuse there, that did not mean they were there to do killing. They could have been there for some other doings, maybe to watch *tiktik mamook memaloose moosmoos*—the making of dead cattle, which were the Indian words for butchering. That was the cut of the defender's point.

Q: What was the health of the Indians at that time?

A: A large number were sick. More than a usual number were dying every day.

Q: Whitman gave them medicines, didn't he?

A: Yes.

Q: Did he give them the same medicines as he did whites?

A: Of course.

Q: Did the Indians know this?

A: They knew that whites died as well as themselves.

Q: But did they know the medicine was the same for both?

A: Doctor Whitman told me that the Indians accused him of giving them different medicines than he gave the whites. They said he was a sorcerer.

Q: When did Whitman tell you this?

A: That morning.

Q: The morning of his death?

A: Yes.

Q: So on that morning, he anticipated immediate danger, true?

A: I don't know.

Q: Did he know whether the Cayuse were planning to kill him?

A: He told me that Tomsucky told him that he would be killed sometime.

Q: Tomsucky said that Whitman would be killed?

A: Yes.

Q: So he knew that the Indians were hostile toward him, true?

A: Doctor Whitman felt insecure at the mission. He was anxious for his safety.

Q: He told you this?

A: Yes.

Q: When?

A: He spoke of it particularly way back in 1845.

Q: How long had you and your family resided at the mission?

A: One month before Whitman's death.

So how could it be that Josiah Osborne heard Whitman say back in 1845 that he felt unsafe, when Josiah was at Waiilatpu for but one month in November 1847? After trial I put that question to him. He told me this: In coming west on the Overland Trail in 1845, he rested up at Waiilatpu before going on to settle in the Valley. That was when he first talked to Whitman. But in 1847 Doctor Whitman came over to the Valley to persuade him to come back to the mission to do some carpentry. Osborne did not want to go. He was doing well in the Valley, and his missus was well along in carrying their fourth child. But Whitman was persistent. So Osborne gave in and took his family back to the mission just a few weeks before the massacre. When they arrived, his missus lost the baby she was carrying. Ten days later their daughter, Salvijane, died of measles. Five days after that, they were in the middle of a massacre. Osborne was still shaking his head about his decision to go back to Waiilatpu.[131]

Whitman had talked a lot of folks into staying on at the mission. And he did it even though he knew that the mission was in danger. He pulled immigrants off the wagons passing through because he needed jobs done at the mission. Fifty days before the massacre, he got Luke Saunders to come teach school and Mister Gilliland to tailor him a suit. Jacob Hoffman was hired for butchering and odd jobs. William Marsh was hired to run the gristmill. Five days before the massacre, James Young was hired to work at the mission sawmill.[132] All of these men were massacred except witness Osborne—who might as well have been.

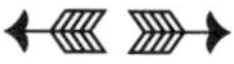

Prosecutor Holbrook told the judge that he would call no more witnesses. That was a surprise. There were many more witnesses he could have put on. In the grand jury proceedings that started two weeks earlier, Holbrook summoned many to testify. The grand jury file shows that the prosecutor issued a call for "Miss Lorinda Bewley, Mrs. Hall, Widow Kimble, Mrs. Husted, Elansin Kinman, Canfield, Miss Mary Marsh, Peter Skien Ogden, Mr. Wm. Mansins Sons two, Eliza Spaulding, Catharine Sager, Eli Young and two sons, Stickers, Youmounis, McKay, Taarken, Tushlape, Oswell, Towattoi, Cumaspellon, Scowlares, Timarcalloutamoux, Mownpou," and others.[133]

Holbrook had summoned more than two dozen witnesses, but only seven had given testimony at the grand jury on the seven indictments. Holbrook called only four of them here at trial.

Some of the witnesses probably never were served with a summons because they were not found. That would be so of the Indian witnesses. Then there were some who did not come down to The Falls because it was just too much trouble or because their heart was no longer strong. The *Spectator* newspaper got its dander up against those who did not honor the call:

> The inquiries of the grand jury progress tardily, on account of the witnesses to come up to the work. Those who shrink or skulk now in the Cayuse affair, will be held to a strict accountability by the public.[134]

Holbrook sat there and leaned back with thumbs in his galluses. Feeling tolerably sure of his case, he rested. He had seven grand jury witnesses ready for trial but decided to call only four. The three he did not call were Miss Catherine Sager, Miss Eliza Spalding, and Missus Mary Husted.

Eliza Spalding, one of the surviving captives, was age twelve when she testified before the grand jury. She later recalled:

> I was nearly as frightened in the courtroom as I was while held prisoner. The lawyers asked such questions about the massacre and the Indians looked so threatening that altogether it was a most unpleasant experience.[135]

Maybe Holbrook did not use her because her heart was shy. But then maybe he did not call her because she might not have been too good at identifying the murderers. She had been new to the mission, a visitor who was not familiar with the Waiilatpu Cayuse. Her father, Reverend Henry Spalding, had left her at Waiilatpu just a few days before the massacre while he and Doctor Whitman went off to see Chief Stickus down on the Umatilla River.[136]

Miss Catherine Sager was Elizabeth's older sister and was age fifteen at the time of trial. She seemed to know more than most about what happened and certainly had plenty to tell in the years following the trial.[137] But Holbrook did not use her at trial.

The best witness of all would have been Missus Mary Saunders Husted, but Holbrook decided against her testimony even though she testified three times before the grand jury. In between the massacre and the trial she married a man named Husted. Her first husband, Luke Saunders, was killed and beheaded in the massacre. She ended up one of the cap-

Eliza (Spalding) Warren   Mary (Saunders) Husted
Catherine (Sager) Pringle

These three survivors of the massacre captivity, shown ca. 1880-1890, were grand jury witnesses but were not called by the prosecution to testify at the plenary trial. (Courtesy Oregon Historical Society.)

tives. She was a strong-hearted, god-fearing woman, who had the pluck to try and calm the savages and keep them from more killing. She kept busy and steadied the other women captives as well. Many years after the trial, she gave a written report of what happened. It was level and sensible and the only account written by a woman captive who was full grown at the time of the massacre.[138]

Why did Holbrook not call Miss Eliza or Miss Catherine or Missus Mary Saunders Husted? Tracking a lawyer's mind is no easy trail, but maybe this was Holbrook's reason: All three of those witnesses were a mite kindly toward their captors. Little Eliza was born and raised among the Nez Perce and thought of Indians as human beings. Missus Husted said, "[T]hey always treated me with decency and respect." Miss Catherine said, "Old Telokite was a man who intended to do right, as far as he knew, . . . [and] was ever after a heart-broken conscience-stricken man. I used to feel sorry for him as I saw him moving about, viewing the wreck of a once happy home."[139]

Elam Young was one of few men who lived through the captivity. His son was killed in the massacre. Holbrook summoned Elam and he answered the call, but Holbrook never used him before either jury. At the time of trial, Elam was settled nearby out on the Twality Plains. He was right there spectating at the trial. But he did not cotton to the way Judge Pratt conducted himself, and maybe that is why Holbrook did not use him as a witness.[140]

Then too, there were some survivors that Holbrook had never bothered to summon to The Falls—not for grand jury or for trial. Two of them were Joseph Smith and his daughter Mary. Holbrook wanted no part of them for his case. The story goes that, during captivity, one of Telokite's sons professed strong love for Mary Smith. Her father urged her to yield to this courting because a marriage would save both of their lives. So the young warrior took her to bed as a wife made willing. She was fifteen years of age at that time.[141]

Whether the story was fair or false, it had been told and retold. For that reason, the testimonies of Mary Smith and her father might not be trusted by those who saw more honor in fatherhood and who sometimes named their daughters Innocence, Chastity, Prudence, and such.

The afternoon was wearing on, but Judge Pratt told the Cayuse lawyers he wanted to finish up the testimony on this day. The jurymen were getting tired; they had already listened to four witnesses since the hour of two. And recollect that at the beginning of the day the defenders told Pratt they needed more time to get ready. Nonetheless, Judge Pratt was of a mind to get all testimony to the jury on this day. He ordered the

Cayuse lawyers to call their first witness. So they did. Their first witness was no less than the Father of Oregon.

He was bent now with age, yet he stood taller than any man in the room. His face was weathered red and stern, but his heart was kind. It was a face shaved clean of any beard, which was not common for those times. Most men had whiskers, and a grown man was hectored when he had none. Straggled hairs on the chin were made game of, as well.[142] Only boys, Indians, and women were cheeked. But of this smooth-faced witness, no one thought the worst, because this was Doctor John McLoughlin, and his manhood was proven. Atop his bones was a mountain cap of snow-white hair. Indians called him *Chakchak*—"White-headed Eagle." He was strong medicine to Indians and was looked up to by settlers as well. Settlers came to think of him as "Father of Oregon" because, as Judge George Henry Williams said, "When the emigrants arrived from the plains poor and needy, he fed the hungry, clothed the naked, and helped them to start life anew in their new homes."[143]

The White-headed Eagle had been living in this wilderness for a quarter part of a century—since 1824, long before most mountain men came, long before any white settlers, and long before many in the courtroom were born. Judge Pratt himself was age four when McLoughlin set roots in the Oregon Country.

McLoughlin had been sent here by the Hudson's Bay Company to be the chief factor at Fort Vancouver, twenty miles to the north. But he had left the Company four years ago to settle down on his claim. His claim was here at The Falls and took up most of the land in these parts, including the very spot where this trial was taking place. He was the founder who had laid out and given away the parcels of land that got this town started. He gave it the name Oregon City.

Being founder, it made him a respected man. But respect is a thing that brings with it the worst in folks. It brings a kind of eat inside. Some here in the Valley and back east in Congress sought to jump McLoughlin's claim through lawmaking. That was a big story in the newspapers alongside of the news of this trial and the news of gold in California. It was the reason why Judge Bryant was not present here to preside in his own court—why Pratt was replacing Bryant. Bryant was busy laying claim to some of McLoughlin's valuable land at The Falls and was back east in Washington City for land-grabbing politics.[144]

So there stood the Father of Oregon swearing oath with his hand over the Bible and Clerk Curry's hand under it. McLoughlin stood a shoulder above Curry, and that silver head was atop of them both. Chief Telokite's eyes wrinkled into the piece of a smile. On this hard frontier, a white man of sixty-six snows was a rare sight.

Secretary Pritchette for the Cayuse began by asking questions aimed to free the air of any wrong notions about McLoughlin and his loyalty. I

Dr. John McLoughlin, ca. 1850s

A witness for the defense. The former chief factor of the Hudson's Bay Company at Fort Vancouver had founded Oregon City, and was widely known as the "Father of Oregon." (Courtesy Oregon Historical Society.)

recollect McLoughlin testifying that he wanted to be an American and had petitioned the government for citizenship. I recollect him saying that he had cut up his claim to The Falls and had deeded away many free parcels in order to make this town called Oregon City. I recollect that Pritchette asked if McLoughlin knew Doctor Marcus Whitman. And McLoughlin said, aye, just as he knew everyone in the courtroom. He said he had known Whitman and his missus since they first came overland to this country back in 1836.[146]

Q: You say you knew Doctor Whitman. Did you ever talk to him about the Cayuse Indians?

A: Aye. In 1840 and 1841 I warned him of the danger in residing among the Cayuse people.

Q: What danger?

A: The danger of giving medicine to them.

Q: Why was that a danger?

A: The Cayuse killed their medicine men.[146]

Q: So what did you advise?

A: I invited Doctor Whitman to come and spend the winter with me at Fort Vancouver and then to go to the Willamette Valley in the spring. I told him that if he would absent himself from the Cayuse for two years, they would then feel his loss and invite him to return. The return could then be made in safety.

That was all Pritchette had to ask of McLoughlin. So the judge told prosecutor Holbrook he could cross-question.

But Holbrook was a surprise. He said he had nothing to ask. I could have been struck down by rainfall, for I thought it was a certainty that Holbrook would return fire at McLoughlin. There were plenty of embers around that Holbrook could have put dry tinder to—smoulderings like hate for squawmen, hate for religions, hate against foreigners, landgrabbers, and the Hudson's Bay Company. Holbrook held a trigger at those hates, and McLoughlin was at the muzzle-end of all of them.

Holbrook might have asked about McLoughlin's half-breed wife. Or he could have reminded the jurymen that McLoughlin was Catholic and the victim was a Protestant missionary. He could have brought out that McLoughlin was still being paid a profit-share from the Company. And he could have let it be heard that McLoughlin's wish to be an American citizen had not yet been recognized by the Union and that McLoughlin was still under allegiance to the Crown and Canada. Then too, it might have done the prosecution some good for the jury to know that McLoughlin was laying claim to The Falls and most of the mills around it.[147] It would have been in dead keeping with Holbrook's nature to ask those kinds of questions.

But then again, maybe the prosecutor was clever by just laying low. McLoughlin's testimony did not come to shucks. McLoughlin testified that he warned Whitman and that Whitman knew the danger. That kind of defense is slim pickings. Murder is still murder even if the victim knows it is coming.

But Pritchette must have felt that his line of defense was a strong position because he pressed it further with his next witness. He called on Chief Istachus. White pioneers called him Stickus. The fact that Stickus was a Cayuse Indian made his testimony a curiosity, and I'll tell you why. If these defendants had not taken Whitman's life but instead had taken his horse, and if Whitman had sued them for stealing, then Stickus would not have been allowed to testify for the defendants. Oregon law said an "Indian shall not be a witness in any court, or in any case against a white person."[148] But in this criminal case, it was all right for Stickus to testify because he was not testifying against a white person. He was testifying against the government. Still, any government that would not let Indians testify must be a government of white persons.

Even though Stickus was a Cayuse, he was from a camp down on the Umatilla River, not defendants' camp up north at Waiilatpu. Stickus was more pleasant than his brothers on trial. Some in the crowd recognized him as the Indian who had helped them on the last leg of their migration across the Blue Mountains. Ever since Whitman had pulled Stickus out of a bad sickness in 1837, Stickus had been Whitman's friend and loyal helper.[149]

Although Judge Pratt allowed Stickus to testify, Pratt did not swear him upon an oath to tell the truth. That might have been because Stickus was not Christianized. An oath upon the Bible would not mean much to a heathen. But the law allowed a witness to be sworn with or without a Bible. And for those who did not like swearing, the law allowed a third way: a witness could "solemnly, sincerely, and truly declare and affirm" to tell the truth. So when Pratt did not require Stickus to do any swearing or affirming, it must be that religion had nothing to do with it. I figure that no oath or declaration was given simply because Stickus was an "Injun."[150]

Stickus knew but just a lick of white language. Even with the help of two interpreters, Pritchette's examination of him was a struggle.

Q: When did you last see Doctor Whitman alive? [*Kunsih mika tahlkie nanitch Doctin Whitman mitlite wind?*]

A: *Klone snow tahlkie. Doctin Whitman kopa nika siwash house kopa Umatilla kopa sun elip yaka memaloose.* [Three snows past. Doctor Whitman is at my lodge on the Umatilla on the sun before he dies.]

Chief Stickus (?), date unknown

A witness for the defense, Stickus was a Cayuse and a friend of Marcus Whitman and other white settlers. The tomahawk he holds is reportedly the murder weapon. The authenticity of the photograph has not been verified. (Courtesy Oregon Historical Society.)

Q: On this day then before he died, did you talk to him about danger at Waiilatpu?

A: Yes. The Doctor is on his horse. He makes to go home to Waiilatpu. I tell him to make care. Bad Indians at Waiilatpu. They talk bad of him. He in danger. They kill him. I tell him these things. He give me good heart and ride away to Waiilatpu.

That was about all Pritchette had to ask. Holbrook had less; he asked just one question.

Q: How did you know Doctor Whitman was in danger?

A: Tomsucky tell me. Tomsucky say they mean to kill Doctor Whitman.[151]

Just like the testimony of McLoughlin, the testimony of Stickus left me shaking my head. To my way of thinking, the testimony did not come to cut whiskers. Maybe Whitman was a damned fool who knew he was riding into wolf jaws, but that was no call to kill him.

But Pritchette was no fool even if Whitman was. Pritchette was secretary of the Territory — second man to Governor Lane. He and Lane knew that, for the good of the Territory, this trial had to be an end of the bad heart between whites and the Cayuse. By putting a Cayuse like Stickus before the public—one who had been friendly to white folks and who had given warning to Whitman—maybe Pritchette hoped that then the settlers would calm down about the whole of the tribe and would see that the massacre was renegade doings. While he was trying to free his defendants, he was also trying to free the Territory of any more hostility. It was time to let things be.

But sad to say, that kind of plotting was of no help to these defendants, because it worked its purpose only if they were hanged. Anything less would just rankle folks all the more. Pritchette was the Territory's secretary and the prisoners' lawyer. He must have been torn by those two calls.

Before Stickus was allowed to leave the witness chair, Pritchette said he had one last question for him.

Q: Tell us, Chief, is it the custom and usage of the Cayuse nation to kill their bad medicine men?

At that, Holbrook was on his feet with an objection, saying that it did not matter what the Cayuse law was. Judge Pratt agreed. He refused to allow such testimony. The jury did not need to hear of savage Indian law.

Pritchette came right back and said, "Defendants except!" This time Pritchette was annoyed by the judge. Judge Pratt's decision was a hard loss for the defense. Pritchette figured that the jury ought to know that what the Cayuse had done was done in keeping with Cayuse nature and custom.

Doctor McLoughlin had already been allowed to testify that "Cayuse killed their medicine men." But now Pratt and Holbrook were saying that jurymen could not be told that it was "custom and usage" to do so. That was a difference as thin as hairs on a snake's belly. It was all right to say that a people were known to do certain acts but not that they had a legal custom to do them.

But even so, what difference would it make to those outside of the wolf pack? You hunt and kill the wolf that brings down your stock. You do it whether the taste of blood is wolf nature or wolf-pack law.

Pritchette called his last witness, Henry Spalding. When Spalding and Marcus Whitman had come west together to set up missions for the Indians, Whitman had gone to the Cayuse at Waiilatpu and Spalding to the Nez Perce at Lapwai. Both were men of the calling, but their likeness ended right there. Spalding was a reverend, Whitman a doctor. Spalding was a stern face with heart to match. His spirit was fixed upon damnation. He was to spend the rest of his life blaming the massacre on Catholics, the Company, and all other evil. He and some other Protestant reverends—John Griffin and William Gray—came down hard on the Pope and priests.[152]

Spalding and Doctor McLoughlin were two at odds, as different as cheese and chalk. Where McLoughlin was commanding, Spalding was crouched. Where McLoughlin was silvered, Spalding was shadowed. Where McLoughlin was at peace with trouble, Spalding was troubled by peace.

Spalding went up to take the oath. His eyes were at corners and went like quirts. He put a sharp gaze on Tom Claiborne. Recollect, those two had quarreled on the street a few days before. Spalding had been pushing his ways on folks about town, and Claiborne took offense.[153] It seemed odd, then, that Pritchette would choose to call Spalding as a witness. Maybe Pritchette was just trying to give a picture of wide support for the defendants. It was, surely so, an unlikely mix of witnesses: a Catholic and Bay Company aristocrat; a Cayuse chief; and now, here, a Protestant missionary firebrand. It was almost too political to be of much good.

Judge Pratt gave the oath; and Spalding answered with pious airs, "I do so swear upon the Holy Evangelists of Almighty God!" Spalding took an oath good. He was a walking oath.[154]

Q: Reverend, you have just heard the testimony of Chief Stickus. Were you present at the Stickus lodge the day before Whitman died?

A: Yes. Reverend Whitman and I had gone to the Stickus lodge together.

The Reverend Henry Harmon Spalding, ca. 1860s (?)

A witness for the defense, Spalding was an ordained Protestant minister and a missionary to the Nez Perce. (Courtesy Oregon Historical Society.)

Q: Did you hear what Stickus told Doctor Whitman?

A: Yes. I too was warned about the danger of traveling back to my mission.

Q: Did you leave with Doctor Whitman?

A: No, I stayed and left the next day after the massacre.[155]

Q: And why did you leave the Stickus lodge?

A: I became fearful and was determined to go home to Nez Perce country.

That was all there was for Spalding. He would sooner have held forth for some sermonizing, but neither Pritchette nor Holbrook had any more for him.

And that was the whole of it. The defenders had no more witnesses, and neither did Holbrook.[156]

It had been a long day. The sun was getting down toward the hills above Robin's Nest across the river. But Pratt said that court was not over yet. He was not ready to make camp until the lawyers made their arguments to the jurymen. His Honor did, however, call a recess.[157] Folks were mighty grateful for that. Womenfolk made for the privies. Most menfolk took to the bushes behind the saloon. The Cayuse had to be told to move off into the woods because an Indian was unashamed when it came to easing nature.

The recess gave time to think about the case made by the defense witnesses. The defense came down to this: Marcus Whitman knew that he was going to be killed; he saw the danger. If that defense counted for anything at all, it only worked on Whitman. It meant nothing for the massacre of all the others. But the defendants were not on trial for the murder of the others. Indictment Eleven was just for the killing of Whitman and not one more.

The Cayuse lawyers missed calling the best witness of all for the defendants. Reverend Henry Kirk White Perkins was his name. Perkins was a good sort, even if he did have four names where most folks got by with two or three. He had been a Methodist missionary at The Dalles and was the only *shuyapu* I knew who understood the massacre from Cayuse moccasins. Perkins told things straight out and wrote this about himself:

> I could as easily have become an Indian as not. I completely sympathized with them in all their plans & feelings. I could gladly have made the wigwam my home for life.

He wrote this about Marcus Whitman:

> [A]n Oregon Indian & he could never get along well to-
> gether. . . . [H]e could never stop to *parley*. It was always
> *yes* or *no*. [H]e was always at work. . . . He looked upon
> them as an inferior race & doomed at no distant day to
> give place to a settlement of enterprising Americans. . . .
> His American feelings . . . were unfortunately suffered to
> predominate. . . . He wanted to see the country settled.

And Perkins wrote this of Narcissa Whitman:

> Mrs. Whitman was not adapted to savage but *civilized*
> life. . . . The natives esteemed her as proud, haughty, as
> *far above them*. . . . She longed for society, *refined soci-
> ety*. . . . She had nothing apparently with them in com-
> mon. She kept in her own original sphere to the last. She
> was not a *missionary* but a woman. . . . And such she died.

And he wrote this about the Cayuse and what they saw happening:

> While [the whites] were rapidly coming in year by year
> and occupying rich lands, [the Cayuse] looked upon the
> Doctor as at the head of the concern. They saw him . . .
> aiding & abetting—planning and directing, & . . . concur-
> ring apparently in their displaceance. What would they
> do? They would do what they did do—"strike for their al-
> tars and their fires." They wanted their *lands*, their
> *homes*, the *graves of their fathers*, their *rich hunting
> grounds & horse ranges*.[158]

I do not know if jurymen would have put any bite in that kind of testi-
mony. And I have been told by lawyers that no judge would have let
Perkins say such things in a court of law. Not relevant, judges would say.
Still, Perkins laid a hand on what was in the heart.

Missionaries and Indians were on a forked trail. Their only rendezvous was a common need for worship. Both had strong heart for what
was holy. But gospel men praised the Creator, and Indians praised the
Creation. To an Indian, Creator and Creation were just different sides of
the same mountain. Missionaries kept those two in twain. Worship was
a quest and a vision for an Indian, but a reverend saw worship as a judgment and reckoning. Where the Indian's heart was fireside and song,
the preacher's was altar and solemn prayer. It was hard to harness the
two in the same yoke because one danced while the other knelt.

It took awhile to get jurymen, prisoners, lawyers, clerks and spectators back in place. Some of the womenfolk had left to get supper on. Some new faces were there because shops were closed now. When all was settled, His Honor called on Holbrook to give the prosecution's summary to the jury. Holbrook was brief. He said what he had to say and sat down.

Then Major Reynolds took a turn for the defense. He was competent, but he did go on some. The newspaper reporter had his pocket timepiece out, and he wrote that Reynolds took forty-five minutes.

Captain Tom Claiborne was not to be outdone. He got to blowing and going something fierce and, as I said, broke two tumblers of water. He outlasted Reynolds by more than twice. The newspaper said that Claiborne took one hour and thirty-seven minutes.

Secretary Pritchette was the best of the lot. He spoke fifteen minutes and said it all.

Then Prosecutor Holbrook was given a second chance—which seemed fair, because defendants had three speeches to his one. Holbrook took twenty-five more minutes. He set the case down plain and convincing: The law says you cannot murder; they murdered; that was all there was to it.[159]

When all of the fist-pounding, finger-stabbing, and tongue-wagging was done, it took better than three hours of argument. It took more time to make speeches about what the witnesses had said than to hear the witnesses say it.

It was time for adjournment, but first the judge told Marshal Meek to keep the jury together and under his charge. Then the judge told the jurymen not to talk to one another or to anyone else about the case.[160] So Meek had to keep two jails now: one for the defendants and one for the jury. The jurymen were not put behind bars, but they might as well have been. They were taken to a boarding place and kept under guard. The judge told everyone to be back in court the next day at the hour of nine in the morning.

Folks were pleased to get home that night. Bellies needed store. It was past supper. Those with a long ride home would have hell to pay with darkness.[161] There was just a sliver of light along the hills west of town. That kind of sunlight behind the mountains had a special meaning to Cayuse. They called it the *edahoe*. But back in Cayuse country the mountains were east, and so the light on the mountains meant a dawning. Here in the Valley, the hills were west. The *edahoe* for these Cayuse on this day at this place was a sundown.[162]

The meals for the jury that night and next morning were slim pickings. Juryman Hunsaker called it a "light diet." Belly hunger was not the only starvation; the jury was starved for talk about the case as well. Even though Pratt told them not to, you can lay to it that twelve pioneers locked up together with bellies empty and minds full would chew and jaw on the testimony.[163] Here's what they might have thought on.

Defense lawyers had put most of their store in one wagon and hauled away at the same sore notion: Whitman knew the danger. The lawyers should have put more shoulder to the fact that there was not much to show that these five defendants were the killers. Witness Chapman said she saw four of them present at some of the killings. But Indians being present at a mission set up to tend Indians is a far holler from taking part in the killings.

As for Tomahas, the one they kept calling "The Murderer," the only other evidence was witness Osborne saying he saw Tomahas carrying arms and stopping Luke Saunders.

As for Clokomas, there was only little Miss Elizabeth Sager saying Clokomas pointed a gun at her sister to tease her.

As for Isiaasheluckas, Miss Elizabeth said she saw him shoot and kill Saunders. But that was not the shooting of Marcus Whitman, which was what this indictment was supposed to be about.

The best evidence was against Chief Telokite alone, but even that had room for doubt. Missus Chapman said she heard his angry voice talking to the Doctor when the shooting happened. Widow Hall said she saw Telokite hit Marcus Whitman with a hatchet, but she saw it from one hundred yards and there were other Indians standing in her way.

The evidence on Kiamasumkin was the most beggared. His name was never mentioned in all of the testimony, except that Missus Chapman said she saw him present there that day.[164]

That weak hitch between killers and the kill would have been something for the jurymen to think about through the night. While the defender lawyers did argue about that lack of evidence, they argued with equal vigor that Cayuse ways called for the killing of bad *tewats* and that Whitman knew it. No doubt both of those barrels could be fired at once. No doubt you can say, "I did not do what I had good cause to do." But no matter how you say it, it still comes out fork-tongued: "Pardon my doing a thing not done." I might have tooth for sweet syrup and stomach for pickled peppers, but to take them in the same bite is no easy swallow.

Then too, the defendants never testified. They were not put in the witness chair to say that they did not take part. Horse sense says if a man did not do a thing, then he ought to stand and say so. But at the same time, the Union Constitution says a man does not have to testify and that nothing is to be taken from that. So how can jurymen be asked to take nothing from what horse sense says means something? That question should have been given careful hands by the judge and the defenders. But it was not.

The Morning of the Fourth Day

It had been a long night for some and too fast for others. But quick or slow, at the hour of nine in the morning, Friday, May 24, 1850, all were back in court. It was the biggest crowd of all four days because doings were down to a reckoning. The jury was finally going to have its say.

But as always in court, other business had to ready the way. After the ceremony of standing for the judge, Deputy Holland read aloud yesterday's page in the Order Book. Judge Pratt approved and signed those minutes.

His Honor then "charged the jury." He did not rush down on them with saber and bugle horn or anything like that. That was not what "charge" meant. The charge was that part of the trial where the judge told the jury about the rules for what they were to do. Pratt instructed about the law and the testimony and took a long time doing it. The newspaper reporter, who was still keeping time, wrote that His Honor took one hour and ten minutes to make his charge.

Tucked away in that charge was one small edge that put a mighty gash into defendants' case. It may have been a mortal wound. The Cayuse lawyers took exception to it. The lawyers put down in the Bill of Exceptions that Pratt's charge told the jury that they

> might infer, that the surrender by the Cayuse nation of
> the Defendants as the murderers of Marcus Whitman
> (the nation knowing best who those murderers were),
> now communicated by the Court as official fact should
> go to the Jury and be received by them as evidence of the
> identity of the accused.

But Judge Pratt said he did not say it that way. So he amended the Bill of Exceptions to show that his charge was this:

> The Court . . . said that on the question of identity, not of
> guilt, it was competent for the jury to consider the fact, of-
> ficially made known, that the Cayuse nation had volun-
> tarily surrendered the prisoners, as the accused, to be
> dealt with according to our laws; and that the Cayuse
> people know best who were the perpetrators of the mas-
> sacre—the fact may go to the jury for what it is worth in
> the matter of identity.

Those two ways of saying it were pretty much cousins. No matter which way it was said, the quick of both is that Pratt was putting into evi-

30

Thursday Afternoon 2 O'clock
Court met pursuant to adjournment.

No 11   United States
         vs
         Telokite et al.

               The Court proceeded
to hear the testimony in the above entitled
Cause, And after having heard the testimony
the Court ordered, that the Jury be kept
together, in charge of the Marshall, Whereupon
the Court gave some special instructions
to said Jury.
              Ordered by Court to adjourn
until 9 O'clock tomorrow morning.

                    O.C. Pratt
                  Judge 2nd Jud. Dis.
                    Oregon Territory

Friday Morning, May 24th 1850.
Court met pursuant to adjournment, the minutes
records of Yesterdays proceedings were read, approved
and signed by the Court. — Present as of Yesterday

No 11   United States
         vs
         Telokite et al.
                    The Court proceeded to hear
the testimony in the above entitled cause, and
after having heard the testimony, and the Jury
being charged by the Court, retired to consider
of their presentments — after a short absence,
returned into Court for the purpose of clearing
some misunderstanding, And after having
heard the witness, again retired to consider of
their presentments. And after a short absence again
returned into Court, And presented through
their foreman the following verdict, that is
to say,
         United States
         vs
         Telokite
         Tomahas (otherwise called the murderer)
         Clokamus
         Isaashelucas
         Kiamasumpkin   } Verdict. —

dence the fact that the free Cayuse, by surrendering these five prisoners, were admitting that the prisoners were the murderers of Whitman.

When Pratt gave that part of the charge, Claiborne's face beat like the heart of a wounded doe and Pritchette sat indignant. There was nothing they could do about it at that time. It was not proper to interrupt the judge during his charge.

Later on when the jury was gone, the defenders had plenty to say to His Honor. They argued that no witness had ever testified that the "Cayuse nation had surrendered the Defendants," and there was no testimony that the Cayuse nation "knew best who those murderers were." The lawyers protested that "the Honorable O.C. Pratt not having been sworn . . . stated the same as evidence." They said that it was something that Pratt had heard others say and was not something that he knew directly. They argued that they had no chance in court to question these "surrenderers." Defendants were being hurt by the outside talk of those who were not eye-to-eye in the courtroom.[165]

Pratt insisted that he was not letting those facts come in to show *guilt* of the defendants, but only to show their *identity*. That was as different as mud and wet dirt. I could not separate it; and, meaning no disrespect to the jurymen, they could not do it, either.

But even if it was proper for the judge to tell the jurymen of the surrender, he might have been wrong about what was meant by it. It was an "official fact" that these five were surrendered to Governor Lane at The Dalles, but there was nothing official or fact about the meaning that Pratt gave to it. Lane asked the tribe for these five defendants by name. Maybe the Cayuse were not saying that these five were murderers. Maybe they were just making peace to stop war on their tribe. Before trial, Chief Telokite told his captors why he surrendered: "Did not your Missionaries tell us Christ died to save his people? So die we to save our people!"[166]

Some say that the five were intended to be only witnesses, not accuseds.[167] Maybe the surrender was just a cooperation with Governor Lane's forces. When a musket is put to a man's throat and he is told to give up his horse and he does it, that does not mean that he surrenders ownership. It was one thing for the jury to learn of surrender, but it was another to read surrender to mean guilt or identity.

Judge Pratt's charge to the jury made it an official fact that the tribe had not just surrendered the defendants but also had fixed them as the murderers. Up until then, there was a weak tie in the prosecution's rope. How was the jury going to hitch Kiamasumkin and the rest of these defendants to the massacre? If that was a dangle in Prosecutor Holbrook's case, then Judge Pratt cinched it down: Defendants were the ones who murdered because their own tribe said so.[168]

His Honor finished his charge and sent the jurymen out to another room to think on their deliverance. So far the jury had done their job by listening, but now they would have their say. When they were ready, the twelve would have to speak as one. There could not be one difference among them—"unanimous" is what Pratt called it. No one was allowed in there with them—no lawyers, no judge, no witnesses, nothing to lead them save whatever they could remember about the charge and the testimony.

No record is kept in a jury room. But afterwards juryman Hunsaker told me what went on behind that door and what had gone on the night before when Pratt ordered them "to be kept together." Right off, all twelve were of the same mind on four of the defendants. But on the fifth, there was argument. On that defendant, Hunsaker stood alone against the other eleven. He believed Kiamasumkin was innocent.

Back in 1846, Kiamasumkin was kind to Hunsaker and his family in leading them over a difficult part of the Overland Trail. It was not easy now for Hunsaker to sit in judgment on an Indian who had been comfort in hard times. So Hunsaker listened with care to the witnesses for some sign that his friend took part in the killing. He heard none. Not one witness had spoken the name Kiamasumkin. Missus Chapman said she saw him present, but Hunsaker questioned her testimony because she was "light-hearted" and did not have a "serious way."

The other eleven jurymen were for quick decision and getting home where they were needed. Hunsaker held fast. It was getting upwards of noon mealtime. As I told before, meals had been none too good or too much since the jury began feed on government time. If a hungry jury was supposed to be quick and sure, Hunsaker was not a good test for that notion. Tempers growled in keep with stomachs, but Hunsaker hunkered down and fixed to hang the jury rather than hang a friend.[169]

So the jury returned to the courtroom with their problem. That was when Judge Pratt called Missus Lorinda Chapman back to the witness chair, which hardly seemed right seeing as how prosecutor Holbrook already had his chance at proof. Missus Chapman then testified that the four defendants she saw present at the mission on the day of the massacre were all "armed with guns and tomahawks." Kiamasumkin was one of the four.

Then Pratt told Hunsaker and the rest of the jurymen this: If Kiamasumkin was present and armed at the mission, that would be enough evidence to find him guilty.[170]

In time, the jury sent word that they had a deliverance. The newspaper reporter had his timepiece out and wrote that the jury was absent a total of one hour and fifteen minutes.[171]

Marshal Meek got everyone in place. The courtroom was packed full. Even Governor Lane was back for the reckoning. Judge Pratt called in the jurymen and asked them if they had a foreman.

Jacob T. Hunsaker, ca. 1850s (?)

The petit juror who for a while was the lone dissenter on the jury. (Courtesy Oregon Historical Society.)

Hiram Straight stood and said that he was voted foreman. Straight was a man of note on this frontier. Back in 1846 he was chosen lawmaker from Clackamas County in the Provisional Government.[172]

Pratt told Straight to read the verdict aloud. Straight did so while the paper shook in his hand:

> "We as Petit Jurors in the above case find the Defendants Telokite Tomahas otherwise called the Murderer Cloko-mas Isiaashelucas and Kiamasumkin Guilty of the charge as set forth in the indictment."[173]

The interpreters gave the news to the defendants. There was a rumble of neighbor talk in the crowd. Judge Pratt gaveled it down before it could break into any kind of "unseemly approval."[174] Then he had each jury-man sign the verdict. Juryman Hunsaker was the third to sign. A heavy heart made his pen slow. He later told me that "he wished he never had agreed to call that Indian guilty—he could not help but doubt."

When the signing was all done, Pratt ordered the verdict to be entered of record. Then he ordered Marshal Meek to take charge of the prisoners and to bring them back at the hour of four in the afternoon for the purpose of hearing sentence passed.

Meek and the militia led the Cayuse back again to the *skookum* house. As soon as they had left, Claiborne was on his feet and asking for "an arrest of judgment," which Pratt at once overruled. Claiborne took exception and then sat down.

Then Secretary Pritchette handed in a paper called a Motion for a New Trial.[175] That motion raised an argument not heard before. Pritchette argued that there was no proof at trial that the crime was committed within the Territory of Oregon or the jurisdiction of the court. Holbrook's four witnesses testified that the killings took place at Waiilatpu—Doctor Whitman's mission—but nobody testified where that mission was situated. So far as the official record was concerned, the mission could have been somewhere east of the Rockies or down in California or up in Canada.

But when Pritchette made that quarrel, there was a groan and shuffling in the crowd. Every settler in the Valley knew that the Whitman Mission was smack in the center of the Oregon Territory.[176] The overland journey from the Missouri cut places into memory like a wagon wheel cut ruts into the trail. But lawyer Pritchette stuck to his guns; there had to be proof of where the crime occurred, and prosecutor Holbrook forgot to prove where the mission was. If the evidence did not show that the murder was committed inside the Oregon Territory, then an Oregon court had no power to try that murder.

United States
v.s.

Selakite
Somakas a murderer
Clokamus
Isaiasshelucas
Kiamasumkin

We as Petit Jurors in the above case find the Defendants Selakite Somakas otherwise called the murderer Clokamus Isaiasshelucas and Kiamasumkin Guilty of the charge as set forth in the indictment.

Oregon City, May 24, 1850

Hiram Straight Forman

Joseph Barnet
J. S. Hunsaker
William A. Cason
Andrew Jackson
Albion Post
Samuel Welch
Joseph Olfney
John Lenamore
Anson Cone
John Ellenburgh
A. B. Holcomb

The Verdict

Signed by each of the petit jurors, dated May 24, 1850. (Courtesy Oregon State Archives, Clackamas County, U.S. District Court Case Records.)

Pratt must have seen that argument coming, because earlier that morning when he gave his charge to the jury, he told them:

> "[T]here is no necessity to prove that the facts given in evidence occurred in the place alleged in the Indictment: it is sufficient that they occurred within the county or other extent of the Court's jurisdiction: if the evidence raises a violent presumption that the offense for which the prisoners are indicted was committed in the District where they are tried, it is sufficient."

Pritchette quarreled with that instruction as well. He said that Pratt's charge was a mistake; Pratt was wrong to allow the jury to make presumptions—"violent" or otherwise—about where the crime was committed.[177]

The judge frowned some and then waved off this new problem like a horsetail swishes at flies. He cured it all with pen and ink. He asked to see Claiborne's record of testimony in the Bill of Exceptions. Where Claiborne had written that "There was no evidence given that the crime charged in the Bill of Indictment was committed in the County of Clackamas," Pratt inserted these words: "other . . . than is found in the testimony of Mrs. Chapman." Then Pratt went to the record of Missus Chapman's testimony; and where she said that she was "at the Mission," Pratt inserted the words, "of Dr. Whitman in Oregon." That was all it took. Now the evidence showed that the crime was "in Oregon."[178]

His Honor then said, "There being no good reason set forth, the Motion is overruled." Secretary Pritchette took exception again and then sat down. He could ride no farther. Pratt had taken his horse.

The Cayuse lawyers had one last chore: they "prayed" for an appeal to the Supreme Court of the Territory of Oregon. That gave Judge Pratt pause. The predicament was this: The territorial supreme court was made up of the three district trial judges. But Judge Bryant had gone east, never to return; Judge Pratt was excluded because his decision was the one being appealed; and judge number three was unknown because word of his appointment had not yet been received on the Oregon frontier. There just was no territorial supreme court to handle an appeal.[179]

But the Act of Congress that created the Oregon Territory government said:

> [A]ppeals shall be allowed in all cases from the final decisions of said district courts to the [territorial] supreme court. . . . [A]ppeals from the final decisions of said supreme court shall be allowed, and may be taken to the supreme court of the United States . . . where the consti-

tution of the United States, or acts of congress . . . is brought in question.[180]

So if no appeal could be taken to the territorial supreme court because it did not exist, then the Union Supreme Court would have been the next place to go. The Union Supreme Court might have done the defendants some good. In later years, that Court showed signs of understanding. At least Judge Matthews of that Court seemed to know the problem afoot when judging one civilization by the laws of another. In 1883 he wrote that white man's law

> is sought to be extended . . . over the members of a community, separated by race, by tradition, by the instincts of a free though savage life. . . . [It] seeks to impose upon them the restraints of an external and unknown code . . . of which they could have no previous warning; which judges them by a standard made by others, and not for them, which . . . makes no allowance for their inability to understand it. It tries them not by their peers, nor by the customs of their people, nor the law of their land, but by superiors of a different race, according to the law of a social state of which they have an imperfect conception, and which is opposed to the traditions of their history, to the habits of their lives, to the strongest prejudices of their savage nature; one which measures the red man's revenge by the maxims of the white man's morality.[181]

But any right of appeal to the Court back in Washington City was a right made of paper that did not serve distant outskirts. Washington City was on the other side of the Union. To cross from one ocean to the other and then back again took one year. There were no jails on the Oregon frontier decent enough to hold five men while an appeal in Washington City was going on.

Having no other place to steer, Pratt struck the words "appeal granted" from Claiborne's Bill of Exceptions. In that way, Pratt did not grant the appeal, but then neither did he deny it. At that point, the defenders could have pressed the judge for a better answer to their prayer for appeal. Claiborne would probably have done so. He was a brevet captain whose rank was won in battle. He knew but one direction—to charge forward. But Secretary Pritchette was a government officer whose rank was won by politics and wait. He knew when to retreat in order to fight another day. Pritchette had in mind one last plan, which I will tell more of later. Pritchette's mind won out over Claiborne's heart. The prayer for appeal went the way of heat from a campfire; it joined the cool of night.[182]

In Mrs Chapman's testimony
On the 4th page in the 4th line from the bottom, after
the word "day" insert the words "armed with guns and
tomahawks"

On the last page strike out the words, "which
appeal is granted", and the signing of the
Bill of Exceptions, tendered to me, will be done
as requested —
May 24th A.D.1850

O. C. Pratt
Judge 2d Jud. Dis.
Oregon Territory —

Trial Judge Amendments to the Bill of Exceptions

The second of two pages, dated May 24, 1850, apparently in the handwriting of Judge Pratt. Note that the judge strikes the language indicating a grant of the appeal but does not insert any language indicating a denial of the appeal. (Courtesy Oregon State Archives, Clackamas County, U.S. District Court Case Records.)

The Afternoon of the Fourth Day

At the hour of four past noon, Friday, May 24, 1850, Governor Lane, the free Cayuse, the defendants, the court people, and all and then some gathered for sentencing. It was a solemn occasion struck with great ceremony. When everyone quieted down, Judge Pratt nodded to Prosecutor Holbrook. Holbrook rose and said, "The United States moves the court for judgment upon the verdict this day rendered and that the final sentence of the law be pronounced upon the . . . defendants."

Judge Pratt then asked of the defendants, "Do you have any reason why sentence should not be passed upon you?"

The interpreters passed that along, and defendants and their lawyers said nothing.

His Honor coughed his throat clear and declared the judgment and sentence of the court:

> "You, Telokite, Tomahas, Clokomas, Isiaasheluckas and Kiamasumkin having been duly convicted by the finding and verdict of the Jury, of the crime of wilful murder as alledged in the indictment . . . are, therefore, each adjudged to suffer death by hanging, and you and each of you are ordered and adjudged to be taken from hence to a place of security and confinement and there kept until Monday the 3d day of June, A.D. 1850, and on that day at the hour of two o'clock in the afternoon, be taken by the Marshal of the District of Oregon, to the gallows or place of execution to be erected in Oregon City, and there by him be hung by the neck, until you are dead. And may God in His Infinite Grace have mercy on your souls."[183]

Reverend George Atkinson wrote in his diary that the sentence was heard with "silence and awe." The crowd "looked feelingly on the adjudged" with "conflicting emotions, pity for the criminals, compassion for those whose friends they murdered, respect for the dead, sorrow that the Indians do not realize it more." It was "a solemn event" done with "perfect order and propriety."[184]

Judge Pratt's reckoning should not have surprised anyone. Governor Lane knew it was coming way back when the defendants were handed over to him at The Dalles. At that surrender, he told the defendants' families to "bid them good bye" because he "did not think that they would ever see them again."[185]

Pratt had to kill them. There was no choice. No penitentiary had yet been built in this new territory. And even if there was a penitentiary, jailing an Indian would be like taking the wings from a bird. Death by hanging was the way it was done, and Pratt ordered it done in ten days.

The reaction of the prisoners was slow in coming because of the interpreters. The prisoners had a hard time understanding the part about gallows and hanging by the neck. They understood whiplashings and cuttings and spearings. Since the coming of the white man, Indians accepted shootings as well. But a choking at the neck was a thing of no honor and was no way to meet the Great Spirit. Three of them "were filled with horror and consternation."[186] But Tomahas stayed as cold as a knife blade, and Chief Telokite took it all with his own kind of grace: "So die we to save our people."

His Honor next gave orders for a death warrant. It was a paper directed to Marshal Meek ordering him to execute the sentence and was "under the name and seal of the Judge."[187]

Verdict was done. Judgment was done. Death warrant was done. Doings were fit and proper. His Honor adjourned. The trial was over.

The Days Before the Execution

The newspaper reporter's article was printed in the *Spectator* a week after the trial. The last paragraph had this to say about Pratt:

> The energy, firmness, and enlightened prudence with which the Judge conducted this trial deserve . . . the warmest expressions of approbation. It is a happy day for Oregon when the administration of Justice is reposed in hands so firm and fearless.

His Honor's hands were "firm," but "fearless" was another matter. He had little to fear. The Cayuse were tamed, the settlers sided with the victims, Governor Lane wanted an execution to end the Cayuse War, and the Territory's only newspaper was pleased as well. The only enemies that Pratt had to be "fearless" about were Pritchette and Claiborne, and their fire was just loud barking from Claiborne and kitten cuffs from Pritchette.

After the trial I talked to a man named Luke Allen. He had been educated in the military and was a man of business in Oregon City. He told me that Pratt was "equal to the emergency." I asked him what he meant by that. He said that Pratt was the right man for the time and place. Later on, Allen wrote that the *emergency* of that time and place was this:

> [The crowd] watched the proceedings with intense anx-
> iety. . . . The bare thought that the five wretches . . .
> might, by any technicality of the law, be allowed to go un-
> punished, was sufficient to disturb.[188]

That was the emergency, and this was how Pratt was equal to it:

> The judge appreciated, in all its seriousness, the respon-
> sibility of his position. He seemed to realize that upon his
> decision hung the lives of thousands of the whites. . . . He
> proved, however, equal to the emergency. . . . His posi-
> tion was dignified, firm, and fearless. His charge was full,
> logical, and concise. . . . [He had] unswerving determi-
> nation that the law should be upheld and enforced.

So the danger was that the prisoners might escape by "technicality of law," and Pratt measured up to the danger by his "determination that the law be upheld." Allen's reasoning was an itch for head scratching. It meant that technicality of law was a thing different from law itself. Thousands of white lives hung on the decision to hang the "five wretches." That was a law of the wild and was much older than any technicality of law born of new civilization.

Allen also wrote:

> If by any chance the Indians had escaped execution, the
> people would have undoubtedly hung them, which act
> . . . would have caused retalliation by the Indians, and the
> situation would have been dreadful, and beyond the
> power of language to describe.

What Allen observed was exactly what the defender lawyers had argued back on Wednesday when they asked Pratt to take the trial out of Oregon City and to hold it up north in Clark County. But it was all too late for that now.

In those days after the trial, there was a quiet buzz and bother among the citizens of Oregon City. Some were grieved that the trial evidence was too loose in tying the five defendants to the massacre. Maybe the real murderers had not been found and convicted.[189]

The *Spectator* newspaper tried to still the gossip. Under a headline saying "Cayuses have Confessed," the *Spectator* printed this:

> We are informed that Telokite now admits that he did
> strike Dr. Whitman with his hatchet, as testified by Mrs.
> Hall;—Tomahas, or The Murderer, admits that he shot

Dr. Whitman. Isiaasheluckas confesses to have shot Mrs. Whitman—and Clokomas, the smallest one of the five, admits that he assisted in dispatching young Sager. But Kiamasumkin says he was present but did not participate in the massacre.[190]

The day before the execution, I met up with Corporal Rob Mahon of Company D. He was one of the Mounted Rifles that was helping Marshal Meek jail the prisoners. Corporal Rob said that the *Spectator* story on the confessions was a heap of lies. He had been with the five Cayuse night and day and they all denied any part in the massacre.[191]

Sam Campbell had a different report. He had got to know all of the defendants on his travels through Cayuse country. He visited them at the island jail while they waited for the hanging. Sam said they were sorrowed by what they did and admitted their savagery.[192]

But Archbishop Blanchet, a man of God high up in the Catholic Church, went ahead and baptized the prisoners and received them into the church. That meant that he must have believed their confessions of innocence.[193]

But then if they denied guilt, why did they not bear witness at trial and do their denying there? It was hard to know who to believe.

Even though there was not going to be any appeal, Secretary Pritchette knew that his job was not done while the five Cayuse lived. If he could not get an appeal for them, he felt bound to fight for pardon. That idea did not set too well with folks, but some were on his side. One of these was Marshal Meek's brother, Stephen.[194] They petitioned the governor for pardon.

A good chance for pardon came when Governor Lane resigned his office and rode off for California directly after the sentencing. Pritchette, second in command, was now in position to take over the duties of governor, including the pardoning power. Pritchette and Marshal Meek were friendly and sided on many political issues. So Pritchette went to the marshal and told him a pardon would be coming. But Judge Pratt told Meek that Pritchette needed patience; Pritchette did not yet have authority. Even though Lane had already gone off to California, he had covered his tracks. His letter said that he was not resigning until June 18, fifteen days after the hanging day. That's when Pritchette argued back that resignation was not the only way he took charge, that he also got powers whenever the governor was out of the Territory. But, said Pratt, there was no evidence that Lane had yet crossed the California border. No matter which way it was cut, Lane was still in charge.[195]

The *Oregon Spectator* newspaper journalist was a minister, an editor, and a Terrritorial legislator. He was probably the author of the 1850 *Spectator* news article reporting the trial events. (Courtesy Oregon Historical Society.)

But Pritchette was determined. On the night before the hanging, he urged Meek to release his prisoners under pardon. The friendship in Joe Meek said he would do anything for Pritchette, but the Union marshal in him said, "I have got in my pocket the death-warrant of them Indians signed by Governor Lane; the marshal will execute them men, as certain as day arrives."[196]

Pritchette should have known that he was trying to stop falling water with a stick. Doings had moved too far along. There was no going back. The five Cayuse would never be set free. Even if they could be pardoned for Doctor Marcus Whitman's murder, there was still all of those other dead victims. Those murder indictments waited there as reinforcements for Holbrook's call-up. If the defendants would not hang for the Doctor's killing, then there was always his missus's killing, Luke Saunders's killing, Frank Sager's killing, and who knows how many more. The Cayuse were headed for either a hanging or long abidings in the *skookum* house, awaiting law done slow and proper.

The Day of the Execution

By and by, the day came—Monday, June 3, 1850. No one would miss a hanging. One thousand, maybe two thousand, were in throng here under a sky that was clear and hot. Womenfolk came as well. Some parents brought their young ones in order to teach them a lesson about crime. Jury Foreman Hiram Straight was there with his daughter.[197]

Some feared that the free Cayuse might try a rescue, so many settlers brought arms and hid them close to the outskirts of town.[198] But there was no call for that alarm because Young Chief Tawatoe and the other free Cayuse were on their way back home, in despair at their brothers' fate and in fear that that fate might become their own.

If Governor Lane would have known about the Cayuse departure, he would have been fuss and holler. Recollect that Lane was of a mind to have the tribe see the hangings "to deter them from similar offenses."[199] But when Lane went south right after the sentencing, Secretary Pritchette told Young Chief Tawatoe that his people were free to return to their home in the ryegrass of eastern Oregon.[200]

The gallows was built down here on the east bank of the Willamette River, just across the bridge from Governor Abernethy Island where the prisoners were jailed. It was set up at the west end of Main Street right there where it makes that turn at what was called the Basin. From the gallows, you could see Doctor McLoughlin's fine house where it used to set just down the way there on Main Street.[201]

The gallows was yellow fir, fresh carpentered with heaps of sawdust all around. Six or seven rough-laddered stairs led up to the scaffold. The scaffold stood just a head taller than the drove of people gathered in close. On top of all of that was a heavy crossbeam going skyward maybe eight feet over the platform. That beam was braced solid because it would be holding the weight of all five prisoners at one time. Probably some spectators were unhappy that there was not to be five separate hangings.

There was no breeze, and the five empty nooses hung still against the sky. They dangled down to two feet off the platform. That meant there would be only a three- or four-foot drop.

The drop rope came down over the crossbeam and forked off to the corners of the trapdoor hinged to the platform. That rope was thick and strong because it had to carry the weight of six—the five prisoners and Marshal Meek doing the fixings.

On whole, the gibbet was a sturdy and efficient contraption for such short use. Still, I had to wonder if a three-foot drop would be enough to break necks.

The gallows stood here in the center of the crowd, rising up as solemn as an altar in church. As far as I know, it was the first gibbet ever built in these parts. A usual hanging was quick, with just a rope over a tree branch. That was the way it was done with the Snoqualmich up in Puget Sound eight months back—tried one day, strung up the next. But civilization had now arrived, so time and effort was put forth to make sure that this execution was being done proper.

The crowd commenced to stir. Someone said, "Here they come!" Folks were on their toes straining their necks to see. One man lifted his child to his shoulders. The hanging party came across the bridge over there. Marshal Meek led the caravan, followed by John Hackett, who was there to help Meek with his duties. Meek was astride a white horse. Stuck down in his belt was a tomahawk—the last piece of gallows. He was not wearing his fancy fooforaw. He was in buckskins. Gone was his strut for this occasion—no merry mountain man. He was all business. Recollect, his young one, Helen, died at Waiilatpu.

Tracking Meek were the Rifles with their prisoners. I could see Corporal Rob of Company D. The five Cayuse were led by Chief Telokite. Two priests were right behind. One of the priests read aloud from the Bible; the other carried a cross. The Cayuse hands were bound in rawhide pieces. Rawhide was probably used in order to save time for a quick burial. Chains would have to be removed and saved.

But even though bound, guarded, and in the company of God men, the Indians were yet a fright to some. As they went by, Missus Barclay, standing over there in the door of her house, fell over in a faint.

When the party reached the gibbet here, Meek and Hackett helped the bound prisoners mount the stairs. That took some time. They·

climbed to the scaffold with new baptized names: Andrew, Peter, John, Paul, and James.

By and by, there were six souls atop the platform, and the crowd could stop straining to see. Meek lined each man next to a noose. One of them begged Meek to use the knife. No Indian wished death by *lope kopa lecoo.* A rope around the neck choked life within. Cutting let life go out.

Then Tomahas did a strange thing. There he was—the big one they called the Murderer, who had sat silent all through the trial with a face that would freeze fire. He lifted his head and spoke in a voice loud enough for hearing yet soft in understanding: *"Wawko sixto wah, wawko sixto wah."* It was a puzzling thing to say because it meant, "Now friends, now friends." It was probably his way of saying that it would soon be over and that Indians and whites could return to good heart.

The trapdoor kept bouncing up and down as Meek moved around on it. The drop ropes grew taut as banjo strings. The crowd whispered and pointed and shifted back and forth on its feet. Two and a half years of wait was coming toward an end.

Meek worked as fast as he could. He put hoods over the prisoners' heads and nooses around their necks. When he was done, he stepped off the trapdoor and took a crumpled paper from his pocket. It was the death warrant, and he was suppose to read it. But Meek was not one for reading; so, as best I recollect, he boomed out, "This here are the warrant to execute! Says these five are to be hung at hour two this afternoon! Says I'm the one to do it! Wal, it are two of the clock and then some, and I'm doing it!" Those may not be his exact words, but they would be his way.

He stepped back, drew the tomahawk from his belt, and, where the drop rope was stretched tight across a brace, chopped at it until it snapped. There was a thwang and a clunk. The cross ropes flayed high into the air. Five bodies went straight down, then yanked up like the lash of a bullwhacker's whip. The priest's voice called out, "Onward, onward to heaven, children; into thy hands, O Lord Jesus, I commend my spirit!"

Three dangled there without motion. Two kicked at the air. One was still shaking after fifteen minutes—probably Clokomas, because he was the smallest of the lot. Meek said it was Tomahas the Murderer; but Tomahas was a big man, so his weight should have snapped the neck. With their faces hooded, it was hard to tell who it was. Whoever it was, his neck did not break, and he was choking. Meek ended the suffering by reaching a foot over and pushing down on the knot. They all swung silent for another fifteen minutes. The crowd around the scaffold moved back. There was a stench of bladder and bowels in the air. Their breath did not come. *Klaska wind halo chako.* They were dead. *Klaska memaloose.*

Sam Campbell whispered the hope to never see another hanging. The crowd began to move off, pieces at a time breaking loose. A few had too much drink and were in high feather, but they did not come to much.

Some lingered on, just standing here and there looking up at the five bodies hanging in the sun. The rejoicers were gone now, off to saloons, I suppose. The gallows were still and quiet—ghostly so. Above the sound of the falls came the crow of a rooster from across the river over there at old Bob Moore's place in Robin's Nest.

I looked into the faces of those who stayed on. I thought to see faces satisfied, hearts made good. But it was not so. It was not the look of pity, either. It was a different look, hard to cipher. I had seen that look before. And then it came to me. It was the look of a hunter standing over the carcass of his quarry after a long day's track—a stare that took the place where hunt had been.

In 1843, seven years before the hanging, folks here made a choice at Champoeg. Joe Meek had called out, "All in favor of an Organization, follow me!"[202] Settlers went to Meek's side and took the first step toward civilized ways. Here, seven years later, with Territory government at hand and trials fit and proper, five souls hanged under a new order of ways to come. It was what folks wanted, what it had all been for, but not without forsaking.

That was the look I saw—forsaking. Not rejoicing, not pitying. It was regret for the passing of old ways. Each step away from wild country makes the heart heavy with forsaking.

Those few old Oregonians left standing here and keeping vigil to old times was the only funeral those savages were to get. The bodies were taken down and carted up Abernethy Road over there across the bridge a half mile or so. There they were buried, still hog-tied, and hundreds of miles from their native ryegrass. Nothing of the fifty Cayuse horses must have been left to go for grave markers because no markers were ever made.[203] Right up to the end, none of it had been the ways of Indians—not the trial, not the hanging, not the burying.

The Days After the Execution

At first the *Spectator* newspaper was unwilling to lay things to rest; it reported that there were yet eight murderers running free. But a month after the hangings, it changed heart and decided to let gone be gone just like Lane wanted it. So it wrote:

> The five Indians, whose trial and condemnation we recorded in our last paper, were hung in the 3d inst., according to the sentence of the court. The execution was

witnessed by a large concourse of people. . . . This closes another act in the sad and terrible tragedy.[204]

Down in California and back in New York, newspapers reported the story. But time and distance made them get most of it wrong:

> In March last, [Governor Lane] formally demanded of the Indians the remainder of the murderers, and nine of them, including two Catholic Priests have been delivered into the possession of the Government of Oregon. By proclamation of the Governor, the Legislature of the Territory was convened on the 13th of May, at Oregon City, to give the prisoners a trial, and our informant thinks that . . . they have been convicted and put to death.[205]

> The popularity of [hanging the accuseds] . . . was undeniable. . . . They were hanged, greatly to the satisfaction of the ladies who had traveled so far to witness the spectacle.[206]

Governor Lane was quick to take his due. He wrote to the Secretary of War:

> I have the honor to report that I have succeeded in bringing to Justice, five Cayuse Indians, being all that are supposed to be living, who were concerned in the murder of Dr. Whitman, family, and others.[207]

Many years after the trial, the massacre took what may have been its last victim. Josiah Osborne's daughter, Nancy, was seven years old at the time she witnessed the massacre. When she was very old, she jumped out of a second-story window and killed herself. She was yelling, "The Indians are coming to kill us!"[208]

That is all I have to tell. It all happened here long ago when these streets and hills and folks had a different look. Yet, whether then and there or here and now, one thing is always the same: When there is heartbreak, there is a thing that yearns to cast blame for it. For the Whitman massacre, the Indians blamed poor medicine, poison, and *iskum illahee*—the taking of land. Holbrook and his grand jury blamed the Cayuse and their savagery. Spalding blamed the Catholics and the Hudson's Bay. McLoughlin blamed Whitman's mule-headedness. Perkins blamed Whitman's patriotism. Pritchette and Claiborne blamed disease, superstition, and Cayuse custom.

But if a blame must be found, then I fix it to be just two different times making merry Rendezvous at first but then, by and by, coming at cross-purpose with each other. One was wild. The other was what the history writer Missus Victor called a *Juggernaut*:

> [T]hese Cayuses were martyrs to a destiny too strong for them, to the Juggernaut of an incomprehensible civiliza-tion, before whose wheels they were compelled to pros-trate themselves, to that relentless law, the survival of the fittest, before which, in spite of religion or science, we all in turn go down.[209]

And yet there is a wonder to know this: When we say the "Whitman Massacre," just what was the massacre? Was it what the Cayuse did? Was it what the trial did? Or was it what the Juggernaut did?

APPENDIX A

BILL OF EXCEPTIONS

The following is a transcript of a document— handwritten, ten pages, on the front and back sides of five sheets of blue stationery (eighth page blank). It is untitled, but, in the last paragraph, is given the name "Bill of Exceptions." It is in the files of the Oregon State Archives in Salem, Oregon. Brackets are here used to indicate words indecipherable in the original.

At a District Court of the United States of America in and for the District of Oregon begun and holden at Oregon City on the thirteenth day of May in the year one thousand eight hundred and fifty by the Hon *ble* O.C. Pratt, Associate Judge ___[?], and during the term thereof there came on to be tried the following cause to wit: The United States of America against—Telokite, Tomahas otherwise called the Murderer Clokomas Isiaahelucas and Kiamasumkin for Murder. And on the 22d day of May in the year [afore]said the said defendants filed a plea to the jurisdiction of the Court alleging that the court had not jurisdiction of the crime charged in the Indictment and setting forth that the crime charged if committed, was not committed within the territory over which the laws and of the United States had been extended at the time of the alleged commission of the said offence.

Which said plea was overruled by the Court, to which opinion of the said Court in overruling said plea and causing the Defendants to answer further the Defendants except. And afterwards to wit: on the 23d day of May in the year aforesaid during the progress of the said trial, at the term aforesaid a jury was impanelled to try said cause and certain witnesses having been introduced on the part of the United States, Mrs. Hall a witness in the said case testified as follows: that on the Twenty ninth day November Eighteen hundred and forty seven she was at the Mission of Marcus Whitman: that the first she saw of the affray, she saw Tilikite one of [End of first page] Defendants striking Marcus Whitman in the face with a hatchet; that she was at this time one hundred yards distant, that she said Whitman was on the ground at the time and about six feet from the Mission house, that witness saw the Indians fighting a man by the name of Hoffman, that Hoffman fell and that then witness started for the Mission house that she found the said Whitman sitting on the sofa in said Mission house—that he was wounded in several places: at the request of Mrs. Whitman she helped take the said Whitman into another room: that at the time [she] saw Tilikite striking the said Whitman there were several Indians standing between her and Tilikite—and that there [were? . . .] a number at the mission the greater portion of whom were not armed—that she did [*sic*: not?] see any of the above named Defendants there except Tilikite: that said Marcus Whitman died at nine o clock at night of the same day: that witness had resided at the Mission three months previous to this time: that the measels prevailed amongst the indians and that many of them died, and that the said Marcus Whitman being a Physician administered medicines to the Indians. That Mrs. Whitman the wife of said Marcus Whitman was shot on the day aforesaid—witness placed Mrs. Whitman on the settee in the Mission House: Tom Sucky came in and told witness she must go home: she had gone about thirty yards—she heard the report of guns and saw a Mr. Rogers throw up his hands. [End of second page]

Miss Sager being called as a witness on the part of the United States testified that she was at the Mission at the time the death of the said Marcus Whitman but that she did not remember the date thereof that an Indian came to her door and enquired for Dr. Whitman. She heard loud talking, she looked and saw guns pointed—heard report of the discharge thereof but does not know who shot the said Dr. Whitman: Witness saw Isiaashelukas one of the Defendants and Tom Sucky an Indian not now here attempting to throw down a Mr. Saunders. that the brother of the Witness was killed: Witness saw Clokamas, the next day after the demise of Dr. Whitman, sitting in the Mission house, laughing and talking a great deal, and that he pointed his gun at her sister as she believes only to frighten her sister. Witness was then ten years of age: that many of the Indians were sick and five or six died each day, and that a large number of the Indians had died; that the said Dr. Whitman had given them medicines: that Jo Lewis was at the mission on the day of the death of Dr. Whitman. [End of third page] that on the evening before [the? that?] death of said Whitman she said Jo Lewis told the witness that he intended to tell the Indians to kill him the said Jo Lewis—to which witness responded that she did not believe him.

Mrs. Chapman being called on behalf of the United States testified that on the twenty ninth of November eighteen hundred and forty seven, she was at the Mission upstairs in bed—heard angry words below in the kitchen—thinks she heard the voice of Tilikite she heard the report of guns—she came down stairs and saw persons bringing the said Dr. Marcus Whitman from the kitchen into the house: that she was certain she heard the voice of Tilikite but did not understand one word he spoke:

that said Tilikite had been the Doctors Interpreter: she did not see the said Tilikite that day but that she recognizes the countenances of all the Defendants as persons present there that day—she saw Tom Sucky there and the sons of Tilikite and J. Lewis: that the latter helped carry Mrs. Whitman into the yard: that Jo Lewis had a gun: that two persons were killed by the [End of fourth page] Indians on the eight day of December eighteen hundred and forty seven by the Indians

Josiah Osborne being called in the said cause testified that on the twenty ninth of November eighteen hundred and forty seven he was at Waiilatpu—heard the report of the discharge of guns; looked out of his house and saw a wounded man pass by whereupon he immediately closed the door and went to the window and saw Tomahas one of the Defendants stopping Mr. Saunders from going towards his family Tomahas was armed: saw Jo Lewis there: Witness secreted himself and family under the floor: whilst under the floor heard the Indians kill Mrs. Whitman Mr. Rogers and a young man: The Indians had assembled for the purpose of killing a beef: a large number of the Indians were sick and an unusual number were dying daily: that the said Marcus Whitman told him on the morning of his death that the Indians accused him of giving them different medicines from those he gave the whites and that the Indians called him the said Whitman a [End of fifth page] Sorcerer: that the said Whitman told witness that he felt insecure at the Mission and that Tom Sucky had told him the said Whitman that he the said Whitman would be killed at some time— Witness had resided at the Mission one month previous to the demise of said Whitman.

Dr. John McLaughlin, having been called on the part of the said Defendants testified that in the year eighteen hundred and forty or eighteen hundred and forty one he warned the said Whitman of his danger in residing among the Cayuse people:—that he invited him to come and spend the winter with him at Vancouver and that in the Spring he the said Whitman could go to the Willamette that if he the said Whitman would absent himself from the said people for two years they would feel his loss and invite him to return which he could do in safety He warned him against giving medicine to Indians as the Indians killed their medicine men. [End of sixth page]

Stickus an Indian Chief being called on the part of the Defendants testified that the said Marcus Whitman was at his lodge on the Umatilla the day before his death: that during the visit of said Whitman he told him that the Indians about the Mission were talking bad about him the said Whitman and that he the said Whitman was in danger.

Here the Defendants Counsel offered to introduce testimony to prove that it was the Custom and usage of the Cayuse nation to kill their bad medicine men:—

The Court refused to admit such testimony to which decision of the Court in refusing to admit the same the defendants except.

There was no evidence given that the crime charged in the Bill of Indictment was committed in the County of Clackamas.

This was all the Evidence given in the cause. [End of seventh page; eighth page is blank]

The Court charged the Jury amongst other things not excepted to as follows to wit "that there is no necessity to prove that the facts given in evidence occurred in the place alleged in the Indictment: it is sufficient that they occurred within the County or other extent of the Courts jurisdiction: if the evidence raises a [violent(?)] presumption that the offence for which the prisoners are indicted was committed in the District where they are tried, it is sufficient"

To which charge of the said Court the Defendants except

The Jury found the Defendants Guilty of the crime of murder as charged in the Bill of Indictment.

The Defendants moved by their Counsel an arrest of Judgment which motion was overruled by the said Court: Whereupon the Defendants by their Counsel moved for a New Trial.

From which decision of the court in refusing to arrest the Judgment and to grant a new [End of ninth page] Trial the Defendants except Pray an appeal to the Supreme Court of the Territory of Oregon: which appeal is granted [under (?) tender (?)] this their Bill of Exceptions which are signed sealed and made part of the Record. [End of tenth page; no signature or seal is appended]

APPENDIX B

COURT AMENDMENTS TO BILL OF EXCEPTIONS

The following is a transcript of a document— handwritten, two pages, on the front and back of one sheet of paper. It is untitled, but the content makes clear that it is Judge O.C. Pratt's amendments to defense counsels' Bill of Exceptions. It is in the files of the Oregon State Archives, Salem, Oregon.

In the testimony of Mrs. Chapman, between the 3d and 4th line thereof, insert the following words. "of Dr. Whitman in Oregon"

In the testimony of Josiah Osborne, in the 3d line thereof, between the word "at" and "Waiilatpu" insert the word "Doctor Whitman mission at"

On the seventh page strike out the last 3 lines, and insert the following "There was no other evidence given that the crime charged in the Bill of Indictment was committed in the county of Clackamas than is found in the testimony of Mrs. Chapman and that of Josiah Osborne"

On the 9th page, strike out all between the 9th and 18th lines and insert the following, "The Court, in its charge, said that on the question of identity, not of guilt, it was competent for the jury to consider the fact, officially made known, that the Cayuse nation had voluntarily surrendered the prisoners, as the accused, to be dealt with according to our laws; and that the Cayuse people know best who were the perpetrators of the massacre—The fact may go to the jury for what it is worth in the matter of identity"

In Mrs. Chapmans testimony On the 4th page in the 4th line from the bottom, after the word "day" insert the word "armed with guns and tomahawks"

On the last page strike out the words, "which appeal is granted," and the signing of the Bill of Exceptions, [tendered?] to me, will be done as requested—

May 24th A.D. 1850

O.C. Pratt
Judge 2d Jud. Dis.
Oregon Territory

APPENDIX C

THE *SPECTATOR* NEWS ARTICLE

The following is a news article from the *Oregon Spectator*,
May 30, 1850, page 2, column 4, and page 3, column 1.

TRIAL OF CAYUSE MURDERERS

Knowing that the public mind is deeply and universally interested in
this trial we give below, a minute and careful report, which we prepared
ourself, expressly for the Spectator. If we do not always express ourself
with legal precision, our legal friends will kindly keep in mind that we
are wholly unused to legal proceedings. Our report, as to the facts of it,
may be relied on as minute and faithful. And we here tender our re-
spectful acknowledgements to Judge Pratt for his kindness in permitting
us to occupy a seat within the bar, for the purpose of taking down the
proceedings of Court.

District Court of the U.S.,   )   His Honor, Judge
Clackamas Co., Oregon T'y.)   Pratt, presiding.
                                         May 21, 1850.

The Grand Jury came into court with an indictment against
TELOKITE, TOMAHAS, (or THE MURDERER,) CLOKOMAS, ISIA-
ASHELUCKAS, and KIAMASUMKIN.

The Indians thus indicted were brought into Court, and the indictment was read in their hearing; and its contents made known to them by
two interpreters, appointed for that purpose. The Court assigned K.
PRITCHETT, Esq., ROB'T B. REYNOLDS, ESQ., and THOMAS CLAI-
BORNE, Esq., as Counsel for the Indians.

AMORY HOLBROOK, Esq. District Attorney of the U.S., on behalf of
the people.

The Court directed the Clerk to furnish the Indians, through their
Counsel, with a copy of the indictment, and the witnesses names en-
dorsed thereof, together with a list of the Petit Jury. Also, the Court ordered that they have said copies two days before they be required to
plead.

Court adjourned till 9 o'clock, to-morrow morning.

————

Wednesday, May 22

9 o'clock, A.M. Court convened. The Counsel in behalf of the Indians appeared, and filed a "plea in bar of jurisdiction," which was verified by the affidavit of Counsel.

The District Attorney made his replication to the foregoing plea in form.

The substance of this plea was that at the time of the massacre the Laws of the United States had not been extended over the Territory of Oregon.

The replication to the plea set forth that all the territory West of the Mississippi, was by the Act of 1841 [*sic*; 1834(?)], embraced within and declared to be Indian Territory; and as such, subject to the laws regulating intercourse with the Indians; and the Act of 1848, creating a Territorial Government for Oregon, gives jurisdiction to this Court to take cognisance of the offence.

His Hon. the Judge, gave a labored and very lucid opinion on the whole matter; and ordered the plea to be over-ruled.

The Counsel for the Indians entered their exceptions to this decision.

The Court demanded of the defendants what further they had to plead. They then made the general issue and plead "Not Guilty."

A petition was then presented to the Court asking a change of venue to Clark county, on the ground of public excitement in this county. This petition was verified by the affidavit of the Counsel for the Indians. Court over-ruled the application.

Two new indictments were here handed in against the same persons, one for the murder of Mrs. Whitman, and the other for the murder of Mr. Saunders; and the same proceedings were had and orders issued as in the case of the other bill.

Court adjourned till 9 o'clock, to-morrow morning.

————

Thursday, May 23.

9 o'clock, A.M. Court convened. Prisoners at the Bar. Counsel for the Indians asked a continuance of the cause. An affidavit was filed, which being deemed insufficient, it was denied by the Court.

The Jury was then impanneled and sworn; twenty persons having been *peremptorily challenged* by the Counsel for the Indians, and two by the District Attorney.

The District Attorney then opened the prosecution with a brief review of the matters in the indictment.

Witnesses were called singly into Court and examined. [We will attempt merely in this place a statement of the most material points to which witnesses testified.]

Mrs. Eliza Hall—being sworn, stated that she was residing at Dr. Whitman's at the time of the massacre, (Nov. 27, 1847.) Hearing the report of many guns, she went to the door of the Mansion house, and saw Telokite strike Dr. Whitman three times with a hatchet,—the blows falling on and about the Dr.'s face. They were in the backyard, about six feet from the door. The two houses were about one hundred yards apart and witness saw and recognized Telokite distinctly. Had resided there three months.

Miss Elizabeth Sager—being sworn, testified that she was residing with Dr. Whitman on the 27th of Nov., 1847, and was then about ten years of age. Saw Dr. Whitman while his wound was being dressed by Mrs. Hall and Mrs. Whitman and at the same time Mrs. W. was shot. Saw Dr. W. next morning, dead. Saw Isiaasheluckas attack and shoot Mr. Saunders, and saw Mr. S. fall where his dead body was found next morning. Saw Clokamas next day with a gun which he pointed at her sister, perhaps jocosely. Had lived at Dr. W.'s four years. There were many sick and dying.—Dr. W. gave medicine to the Indians.

Mrs. Lorinda Chapman—being sworn, testified that being at Dr. Whitman's on the 27th Nov., 1847, she was in bed sick above stairs. Heard loud and angry talking in the kitchen and recognized the speaker's voice distinctly as that of Telokite.— Knew his voice from hearing him rehearse for Dr. Whitman. Heard guns and confusion and went down stairs, and there saw Dr. W. wounded by a a cut across the face. Started, in company with Mr. Rogers and Mrs. Whitman, to go to the Mansion House and at the kitchen door Mr. R. and Mrs. W. were killed. Could not stir with alarm. While standing there, saw the four prisoners at the Bar, armed—recollects them distinctly: did not see Telokite. Dr. Whitman was alive when she left. Saw the Indians rolling his dead body about next morning. There were many sick and Dr. W. gave medicine.

Mr. Josiah Osborn—being sworn, testified that he was at Waiilatpu on Nov. 27, 1847, was sick in Dr. W.'s house. Heard guns and went to the door and saw Mr. Kimble running and wounded, retreated inside and through the window saw Tomahas pursuing Mr. Saunders. While under the floor with his family heard murder going on. Dr. Whitman gave the same medicine to both Indians and Whites. Know Dr. W. was a white American citizen. Mansion House door was three feet high from the ground. The Indians knew that the Whites died as well as themselves. Dr. W. was anxious as to his safety, and spoke of it particularly in 1845. Does not know whether the Dr. anticipated immediate danger.

The District Attorney here said that he would call no more witnesses except to rebut testimony in the defence.

Testimony for the defence being called,

Dr. John McLaughlin—being sworn, testified that he had warned Dr.

Whitman of danger in 1840 and 1841, as the Indians did kill their own medicine men.

Stickas—(a Cayuse Indian) called, and through two interpreters testified that Dr. W. left his lodge on the Utilla the day before the Massacre to go home, and after the Dr. was on his horse he told him to be careful for the bad Indians would kill him. The Dr. thanked him and left. Tomsuckee told Stickas they were going to kill Dr. W.

Rev. Henry H. Spaulding—was sworn, and testified that he was at Stickas' lodge with Dr. W. and had similar warnings and the next day after the massacre became so fearful that he determined to go home to the Nes Perces country.

Here the testimony closed, and the District Attorney gave a brief summary of the evidence to the Jury.

Maj. R.B. Reynolds opened the defence in an address, the delivery of which occupied some 45 minutes.

Capt. T. Claiborne next addressed the Jury for one hour and thirty-seven minutes.

K. Prichette, Esq., closed the defence in an appropriate concluding appeal of some fifteen minutes' length.

The District Attorney then closed the prosecution in a neat, condensed, and forcible presentation of the whole subject. This address occupied twenty-five minutes.

Court adjourned till 9 o'clock, to-morrow morning.

Friday, May 24.

Court convened. Prisoners at the Bar, and the Jury in their place.

His Honor the Judge then gave his Charge to the Jury. The Charge was full, clear, and satisfactory, both in reference to the law and the testimony; and its delivery occupied one hour and ten minutes.

Jury retired and after an absence of one hour and fifteen minutes, returned a verdict against the prisoners—that they were guilty as charged.

Counsel for the Indians moved the Court in arrest of judgment—which was overruled.

A new trial was then moved for. Which was also overruled.

Court took a recess till 4 o'clock, P.M., at which time, having again convened, His Honor the Judge pronounced the final sentence of the law on the prisoners; and adjudged that they be hung on Monday, the 3d day of June, at the hour of 2 o'clock, P.M.

SENTENCE

You, *Telokite, Tomahas, Clokomas, Isiaasheluckas* and *Kiamasumkin,* having been duly convicted by the finding and verdict of the Jury, of the crime of wilful murder as alledged in the indictment, are therefore each adjudged to suffer death by hanging, and you and each of you are ordered and adjudged to be taken from hence to a place of security and confinement, and there kept until Monday the 3d day of June, A.D. 1850, and on that day at the hour of two o'clock in the afternoon, be taken by the Marshal of the District of Oregon, to the gallows or place of execution to be erected in Oregon City, and there by him be hung by the neck, until you are dead.

And may God in His Infinite Grace have mercy on your souls.

———

This closes the narrative of the proceedings in this case, but before we leave the subject we wish to make one or two remarks. The circumstances attending this trial reflect the highest degree of credit on the people of this Territory. It is scarcely possible that more intense feeling could possess every bosom than has prevailed here in regard to this trial. And yet it all passed off with the most perfect quiet. From two hundred to three hundred persons were present during the trial but never in a single instance did we, witness the slightest impropriety of conduct. The solemnity and stillness of a church characterised the court room during the whole proceeding.

We cannot, however, leave this matter without giving expression to the strong and universal feeling of admiration which prevails with reference to the conduct of Judge Pratt in this trial. The energy, firmness, and enlightened prudence with which the Judge conducted this trial deserve, as they have elicited, the warmest expressions of approbation. It is a happy day for Oregon when the administration of Justice is reposed in hands so firm and fearless.

APPENDIX D

THE TRIAL JUDGE'S TWELVE RULINGS

During the course of the Whitman Massacre trial, Judge Orville C. Pratt made twelve rulings that might have been potential assignments of error on appeal if such a review had been granted. They were as follows:

1. Denial of the defendant's Plea in Bar alleging no court jurisdiction.

2. Denial of the defendant's Petition to Change the Venue to Clark County.

3. Denial of defendant's Motion for Continuance pending the subpoena of defense witness Quishem.

4. Denial of defendant's proffered evidence of the Cayuse custom of killing ineffective medicine men.

5. Taking judicial notice (without any evidence thereof) of the fact that the Cayuse tribe had voluntarily surrendered the prisoners to Governor Lane and the militia and that the tribe knew best who were the perpetrators.

6. Instructing the jury that the tribe's voluntary surrender of the prisoners might be used by the jury as evidence of the identity of the perpetrators.

7. Allowing a prosecution witness to testify a second time after the jury had begun its deliberations.

8. Instructing the jury that if the defendants were present and armed at the mission on the day of the murder, that would be sufficient to find the guilt of each of them.

9. Denial of defendants' Motion for an Arrest of Judgment.

10. Denial of defendants' Motion for a New Trial based upon the lack of any evidence showing that the murder occurred within the Oregon Territory.

11. Amending the Bill of Exceptions to read that prosecution witness Chapman had testified that the Whitman Mission was "in Oregon."

12. Denying the defendants' prayer for an appeal.

NOTES

The *Oregon Historical Quarterly* appears below as *OHQ*; the *Quarterly of the Oregon Historical Society* as *QOHS*; the Oregon Historical Society, Portland, Oregon, as OHS.

1. J.R. Cardwell, "The First Fruits of the Land," *QOHS* 7 (1906) 34-35; Hubert Howe Bancroft, *History of Oregon*, 2 vols. (San Francisco, 1886-88) 1:637; *Yester-years of Morrow* (Heppner, Oreg., 1959) 10.

2. In 1844 some of the eastern press had this to say about the "forlorn" Oregon Country: "[I]t is one of the least favored of heaven . . . the mere riddlings of creation . . . barren as the desert . . . unhealthy . . . a country to which to banish its rogues and scoundrels . . . the most irreclaimable barren wastes of which we have read, except the desert of Sahara." Quoted in *McKay v. Campbell*, 16 Fed. Cas. 161, 163 (1871). Some reports show that the 1850 population in the Oregon Territory comprised 5,400 males and 3,600 females. J. Kenneth Mumford, "Newcomers in a New Land," in Richard M. Highsmith and A. Jon Kimerling, *Atlas of the Pacific Northwest*, 6th ed. (Corvallis, Oreg., 1979) 15. And see Bancroft, *History of Oregon*, 2:66 n.1. Frances Fuller Victor is acknowledged to be the incipient author of the second volume of Bancroft's *History of Oregon*. William Alfred Morris, "The Origin and Authorship of the Bancroft Pacific States Publications: A History of a History," *QOHS* 4 (1903) 352. But see note 188, infra. Concerning the spray and noise from the Falls, see Andrew Dominique Pambrun, *Sixty Years on the Frontier in the Pacific Northwest* (Fairfield, Wash., 1978) 78-79.

3. In 1850 other small settlements existed along the Willamette River within a five-mile range of Oregon City, among them Milwaukie, Clackamas City, Green Point, Linn City (Robin's Nest), Multnomah City, and Falls City (Canemah). White population of the entire Falls area was 1,200. Howard McKinley Corning, *Willamette Landings*, 2d ed. (Portland, 1973) 30-61.

4. The Thomas Jefferson Hubbard proceedings on July 4, 1835, at Fort William on Sauvie Island were more like a coroner's inquest than a trial. Hubbard was given a written certificate showing "justifiable homicide" and went on to become one of the prime movers in establishing Oregon's Provisional Government. William H. Gray reported that a "Rev. Mr. Leslie" presided as judge, but Bancroft calls that report erroneous. The naturalist John Kirk Townsend, who sat as a "juror," reported the incident in his *Narrative of a Journey Across the Rocky Mountains to the Columbia River* (1839; reprint, Omaha, 1978) 223-24. See Bancroft, *Oregon*, 1:76, 95 n.26; William H. Gray, *History of Oregon, 1792-1849, Drawn from Personal Observation and Authentic Information* (Portland, 1870) 198; Oswald West, "First White Settlers on French Prairie," *OHQ* 43 (1942) 204; Leslie M. Scott, "Modern Fallacies of Champoeg," *OHQ* 32 (1931) 214; Matthew P. Deady, *Pharisee Among Philistines, The Diary of Matthew P. Deady, 1871-1892*, ed. Malcolm Clark, Jr. (Portland, 1975) 107.

5. *Oregon Spectator*, May 30, 1850. Hubert Howe Bancroft reports there were between four hundred and five hundred onlookers. Idem, *Chronicles of the Builders of the Commonwealth*, 2 vols. (San Francisco, 1891-92) 2:245. In 1852

the *Oregonian* raised the question of the "dangerous experiment" of women's lifting their dresses while negotiating puddles. Terence O'Donnell and Thomas Vaughan, *Portland: An Informal History and Guide* (Portland, 1976) 13.

6. There is no historical record as to the room used for the trial. But it was probably indoors, because the *Spectator* article of May 30, 1850, refers to a "courtroom." Jacob Hawn's tavern in Lafayette, Oregon, had been the scene of trials. Sidney Teiser, "First Associate Justice of the Oregon Territory: Orville C. Pratt," *OHQ* 49 (1948) 178. An Oregon City trial conducted immediately before the Cayuse murder trial involved a stairway and a second story. Frances Fuller Victor, *The River of the West*, ed. Winfred Blevins (Missoula, 1983) 2:259-60, 370n. *History of the Bench and Bar of Oregon* (Portland, 1910) 37; Harvey E. Tobie, *No Man Like Joe* (1949) 145, 204.

7. Clifford M. Drury, *Marcus and Narcissa Whitman and the Opening of Old Oregon*, 2 vols. (Seattle, 1973) 1:228, 2:331. Pritchette to Abernethy, May 26, 1850, OHS Ms. 929.

8. There is no direct evidence that Governor Lane was present at the trial. But he lived at Oregon City, the territorial capital, and was in town at the time, as is known from certain correspondence. See, for example, Lane to Orlando Brown, May 25, 1850, Oregon City, and to the Secretary of War, May 27, 1850, Oregon City, OHS Ms. 1146, Box 5. Knowing the extreme significance that Lane attached to the trial, it is unlikely that he did not make periodic appearances in the courtroom.

In light of Lane's character, we may also assume that the free Cayuse were not voluntary spectators at the trial. Pritchette to Abernethy, May 26, 1850, OHS Ms. 929.

9. Lane to Secretary of War, October 22, 1849, OHS Ms. 1146, Box 5. And see Charles H. Carey, *A General History of Oregon Prior to 1861* (Portland, 1935) 563 n.26.

10. *Spectator*, March 24 and April 4, 1850; and see text at note 58, infra.

11. Lane to Secretary of War, October 22, 1849, OHS Ms. 1146, Box 5. And see James E. Hendrickson, *Joe Lane in Oregon: Machine Politics and the Sectional Crisis, 1849-1861* (New Haven, 1967) 14.

12. Bancroft, *Oregon*, 2:83, 88-89; *Spectator*, April 18, 1850; Ray Glassley, *Pacific Northwest Indian Wars* (Portland, 1953) 46; Raymond Settle, ed., *The March of the Mounted Riflemen* (Lincoln, Neb., 1989) 13, 16, 21, 22, 371.

13. Theodore Stern, Martin Schmitt, Alphonse Halfmoon, "A Cayuse-Nez Perce Sketchbook," *OHQ* 81 (1980) 350-51. By 1850 some Cayuse had begun to wear items of pioneer dress such as frock coats, vests, cotton shirts, and felt hats. See also Narcissa Whitman to Stephen and Clarissa Prentiss, March 30, 1837, in *Transactions of the Oregon Pioneer Association, 1891* (Portland, 1893) 94.

14. *Spectator*, May 30, 1850; Drury, *Marcus and Narcissa Whitman*, 2:175-77; Samuel L. Campbell, *Autobiography of Samuel L. Campbell, Frontiersman and Oregon Pioneer*, ed. Rowena Campbell Grant (Mannford, Okla., 1984) 52, 129, 133, 243. Another drawing of Telokite by Paul Kane shows a much younger-looking Telokite. See Erwin N. Thompson, *Shallow Grave at Waiilatpu: the Sagers' West*, 2d ed. (Portland, 1985) 96.

15. Lane, Report to the Secretary of War, October 22, 1849, OHS Ms. 1146, Box 5; Townsend, *Narrative of a Journey.*

16. Myron Eells, *Marcus Whitman, Pathfinder and Patriot* (Seattle, 1909) 96. The census was taken by Anson Dart, the superintendent for Indian Affairs in Oregon.

17. *Reader's Encyclopedia of the American West*, s.v. "Oregon" and "Oregon Trail." Phonetic English spelling of spoken Native American languages varies widely. The Cayuse word for "white people" is variously spelled. Clifford Drury spells it *suapies* and reports that it literally means "the people who wear high hats." *Marcus and Narcissa Whitman*, 1:192 n.4. The museum exhibits at the Whitman Mission National Historic Site near Walla Walla spell the word *suyapos*. The Chinook Jargon word is *seahpo*. In this work, the author uses *shuyapu* because the suffix, *-pu*, accords with analysis of the name *Waiilatpu* and the spelling more closely indicates the probable pronunciation. See note 36, infra.

18. Bancroft, *Oregon*, 2:96; Lewis A. McArthur, *Oregon Geographic Names*, 5th ed. (Portland, 1982); Peter C. Watts, *Dictionary of the Old West, 1850-1900* (New York, 1977) 301.

19. Carey, *General History*, 556, 563.

20. For more detailed accounts of this "capture" and delivery, see Drury, *Marcus and Narcissa Whitman*, 2:321-25; Bancroft, *Oregon*, 2:94; Malcolm Clark, Jr., *Eden Seekers: The Settlements of Oregon, 1818-1862* (Boston, 1981) 234; Priscilla Knuth, "Picturesque Frontier: The Army's Fort Dalles," *OHQ* 67 (1966) 297; Robert H. Ruby and John A. Brown, *Indians of the Pacific Northwest: A History* (Norman, 1981) 103-5; Hendrickson, *Joe Lane*, 14-16; *Spectator*, April 18, May 2, 1850. Lane's correspondence orchestrating the Cayuse surrender may be found in OHS Ms. 1146, Box 5.

21. Curry to Thurston, April 20, 1850, OHS Ms. 700; Bancroft, *Oregon*, 2:348-49; Tobie, *No Man Like Joe*, 185; Eva Emery Dye, "Boone Family Reminiscences as Told to Mrs. Dye," *OHQ* 42 (1941) 223, 226 (Curry always worked in rolled-up shirtsleeves and wore a high hat). File, *United States v. Telokite* lists Curry throughout as "Clerk." See also text at note 46, infra.

22. *Spectator*, May 30, 1850. This article covers almost two full-length columns and is set forth in full in Appendix C. Like Holland's Order Book, it is a primary research tool for much of the detail in this book. Emphasis and trust are placed on the reporter's claim that the account was *"minute* and *careful . . .* and *faithful."*

It is possible that the reporter was the Reverend Wilson Blain, the *Spectator's* editor in chief from October 1849 to September 1850. There is no evidence as to whether the *Spectator* had a staff of reporters at the time. In the mid-1850s, it was a four-column, four-page, semimonthly publication. Blain could probably have handled all the major local news reporting, with occasional help from free-lance stringers on news of obituaries, marriages, recipes, anniversaries, picnics, and other short items. On the other hand, as he was a Protestant minister and a member of the Territorial Legislature then in session in Oregon City, he may have arranged for someone else to report the trial. George S. Turnbull, *History of Oregon Newspapers* (Portland, 1939) 27-28, 45-46; George H. Himes, "History of the Press of Oregon," *QOHS* 3 (1902) 353-55.

23. Although the record shows that two interpreters were needed, nowhere does it verify the use of a double translation through the intermediate Chinook Jargon. However, the practice was employed in other official government dealings with the Indians (T.T. Geer, *Fifty Years in Oregon* [New York, 1912] 205, quoting James Nesmith's account of treaty negotiations with the Rogue River Indians), and may therefore have been used at trial. It would be one explanation for why two interpreters were needed. Needless to say, much would be lost in the translation of complex legal verbiage over such double relay. The Chinook Jargon used throughout this book is taken from Edward Harper Thomas, *Chinook: A History and Dictionary of the Northwest Coast Trade Jargon*, 2d ed. (Portland, 1970).

24. Clark, *Eden Seekers*, 271-72.

25. Ibid. at 243-44. See also Frances Fuller Victor, *The River of the West* (Hartford, Conn., and Toledo, Ohio, 1870) 505-6; Tobie, *No Man Like Joe*, 210-12.

26. Victor, *The River of the West*, 321.

27. Pratt, Holbrook and Curry were all thirty or thirty-one years old; Meek was forty; Lane was fifty. There is no way of knowing the age of the Cayuse. *Tyee* means chief. *Hyas tyee* is a big chief. The *Saghalie Tyee* is the heavenly chief—God, or the Great Spirit.

28. *History of Bench and Bar*, 273; Teiser, "Orville Pratt," 174-78.

29. Teiser, "Orville Pratt," 180-81, 191; Victor, *River of the West*, 497-98.

30. We do not know if Judge Pratt was graced that day by a judicial robe of office. But if any such robe were available on the frontier, Pratt would have worn it. In later years, he was known to touch up his graying temples with shoe blackener. Deady, *Pharisee Among Philistines*, xxvi.

31. Teiser, "Orville Pratt," 176-77, 180, 188; Tobie, *No Man Like Joe*, 203.

32. *Spectator*, May 30, 1850; Elam Young to Thurston, July 24, 1850, in Tobie, *No Man Like Joe*, 203-4, 303 n.1. Historians are likewise mixed in their assessment of Pratt's contribution to the Oregon court system. Tobie claimed that "He laid the foundation for the Oregon judiciary," but Teiser, in "Orville Pratt," 191, wrote that he "left little permanent impress upon Oregon's . . . judicial history."

A flattering biography of Pratt is given in Bancroft, *Chronicles of the Builders*, 2:232, but the glow in this account is partly explained by the fact that Pratt paid Bancroft $2,600 to write it. John W. Caughey, *Hubert Howe Bancroft, Historian of the West* (Berkeley and Los Angeles, 1946) 323. For example, according to Sidney Teiser, Bancroft's *Chronicles* reports that Pratt married a Mrs. Lizzie Jones, but says nothing of the fact that that marriage followed a stormy divorce from Pratt's first wife, who charged as grounds Pratt's adultery with Mrs. Jones. "Orville Pratt," 188-89.

33. We know that Indictment Eleven was read aloud. Customarily it would have been read by Holbrook or Curry or Holland, but, since it appears to be written in Holland's clear hand, it is likely that he read it.

34. The witnesses who appeared before the grand jury were "Catherine Sager, Elisabeth Sager, Eliza Hall, Mary Husted, and Lorinda Chapman"—all women. Indictment Eleven, which is in File, *United States v. Telokite*, is quoted in full in

Robert H. Ruby and John A. Brown, *The Cayuse Indians: Imperial Tribesmen of Old Oregon* (1972, Norman) 303.

35. Campbell, *Autobiography*, 52, 129, 133, 243; Drury, *Marcus and Narcissa Whitman*, 2:253 n.103. Nard Jones, in *The Great Command, the Story of Marcus and Narcissa Whitman and the Oregon Country Pioneers* (New York, 1959) 240, says the name *Tomahas* means "murderer," while Stanley Vestal says it means "pierced by throwing" (*Joe Meek* [Caldwell, Idaho, 1952] 311). Vestal is more likely correct. Today, a good defense lawyer would have successfully objected to any such prejudicial reference, whether it were a disparagement, a sobriquet, or a translation.

36. For her helpful assistance on translation, the author is indebted to Marjorie Williams Waheneka, a park ranger at the Whitman Mission National Historic Site. Ms. Waheneka is a member of the Umatilla Confederated Tribes and has taught the Cayuse-Nez Perce-Sahaptin language on the Umatilla Reservation at Pendleton, Oregon.

37. Whitman's words in this fictionalized conversation with the narrator are taken from Whitman's letter to his parents, dated May 16, 1844, in Archer Butler Hulbert and Dorothy Printup Hulbert, *Marcus Whitman, Crusader*, vols. 6-8 of *Overland to the Pacific* (Denver, 1936-41) 8:98-99.

Much has been written about the life of Marcus Whitman. The early works include Oliver W. Nixon, *How Marcus Whitman Saved Oregon* (Chicago, 1895) and Eells, *Marcus Whitman, Pathfinder and Patriot*. Among the more recent works are Hulbert, *Marcus Whitman, Crusader*, and Jones, *The Great Command*. Unquestionably the definitive work is Drury, *Marcus and Narcissa Whitman*.

38. Thompson, *Shallow Grave*, 41-42 and n.84; Drury, *Marcus and Narcissa Whitman*, 2:202.

39. See maps, Ruby and Brown, *Indians*, 39, 69.

40. Ruby and Brown, *The Cayuse*, 3. And see Jarold Ramsey, comp. and ed., *Coyote Was Going There, Indian Literature of the Oregon Country* (Seattle and London, 1977) 15.

41. National Geographic Society, *The World of the American Indian* (Washington, D.C., 1974) 245.

42. Gray, *History of Oregon*, 228. Concerning the negotiations for the Elijah White code, see Drury, *Marcus and Narcissa Whitman*, 2:20-23; Hulbert, *Marcus Whitman, Crusader*, 8:16-19.

43. The Organic Law of the Provisional Government of Oregon of 1845 may be found in *General Laws of Oregon, 1843-1872* (Salem, 1874) 46-51. The 1843 Organic Law may be found in "The Oregon Archives, 1841-1843," ed. David C. Duniway and Neil R. Riggs, *OHQ* 60 (1959) 256-62. The state of the law of Oregon's Provisional Government and the adoption of the 1839 statutes of the Iowa Territory are more fully explored in Arthur S. Beardsley, *Code Making in Early Oregon* (1936; reprint, Seattle, 1936) 1-8; Lawrence T. Harris, "History of Oregon Code," *Oregon Law Review* 1 (1922) 134-41; Robert S. Hunt, "Law and Land in a Stateless Society," *Wisconsin Law Review* (1980) 1194-99.

The narrator's reference to James A. O'Neil's copy of the 1839 Iowa statutes book is a surmise not fully documented by history. Some contend that Elijah White's copy of that book may have led to Oregon's incorporation of Iowa law. Hunt, "Law and Land," 1196; Beardsley, *Code Making*, 7. But in September 1843, the Provisional Government lawmakers did pay O'Neil $10.50 for his Iowa statute book. Duniway and Riggs, "Oregon Archives," 272; and see F.G. Young, "Financial History of Oregon," *QOHS* 7 (1906) 394. The important point seems certain: Law books in the far frontier in the 1840s must have been scarce, and lawmakers would be strongly persuaded to adopt any code ready at hand and in embodiment. Hunt, "Law and Land," 1212.

These early Oregon lawmakers must have had at their disposal a copy of the Articles of Compact of 1787, an ordinance of Congress established to govern the Ohio Territory (1 Stat. 51), because much of the language of the Oregon Provisional Government's Organic Law is an exact copy of that 1787 Compact. Compare Organic Law with Articles of Compact in *General Laws of Oregon*, 46 *et seq.*, and 59-60n. See also William D. Fenton, "The Winning of the Oregon Country," *QOHS* 6 (1905) 351.

Another potential source for the proscription against murder might have been an enactment of the First Congress in 1790, which stated:

> [I]f any person or persons shall within . . . any other place or district of country, under the sole and exclusive jurisdiction of the United States, commit the crime of wilful murder, such person or persons on being convicted shall suffer death.

1 U.S. Stat. at Large 112 (April 30, 1790). But the use of that statute would have been troubled by the question of whether in 1847—the year of the murder—the federal government had "sole and exclusive jurisdiction" in Oregon. See text at notes 75-79, infra.

44. Act to Establish the Territorial Government of Oregon, 9 Stat. 323 (1848), in *General Laws of Oregon*, 52-63.

45. *Revised Statute Laws of the Territory of Iowa, 1839 (Little Bluebook)*; *Revised Statutes of the Territory of Iowa (Big Bluebook)*. See *History of Bench and Bar*, 263; Beardsley, *Code Making*, 8. That Chapman had a copy of the *Big Bluebook* is a strong likelihood.

46. Concerning the battle of the *Bluebooks* and the involvement of Holbrook, Pratt and Curry, see Beardsley, *Code Making*, 8-12, 1517; Clark, *Eden Seekers*, 251; Teiser, "Orville Pratt ," 183; Curry to Thurston, April 20, 1850, OHS Ms. 700; Bancroft, *Oregon*, 2:297.

Lane called a special session of the Oregon Territorial Legislative Assembly to meet in Oregon City on May 6, 1850. *General Laws of Oregon*, 60, n.1. It was at that time that Curry and Buck were appointed to compile and publish the "Twenty Acts." Beardsley, *Code Making*, 15. Curry was a logical appointment because he had been an editor of the *Spectator* and had published the short-lived rival newspaper, the *Free Press*. Clark, *Eden Seekers*, 189-90; Tobie, *No Man Like Joe*, 185.

The handbook entitled *Twenty Acts—Editors Curry & Buck* (Oregon City, 1850) was Oregon's first *printed* law code. Thus, shortly before the trial no laws were readily accessible for court research. This would have been a good reason to have the presence of Curry and his amassed materials at the trial and, in turn, to bring him back into service as court clerk even though, just one month previously, he had written of his retirement to farming. See text at note 21, supra.

47. Compare the chapters entitled "Crimes and Punishments" in *Little Bluebook*, 142, and *Big Bluebook*, 165-66.

48. *Nash v. State*, 2 Iowa 286 (1849) 290.

49. Beardsley, *Code Making*, 12.

50. Clark, *Eden Seekers*, 155, 170, 241; Percy Maddux, *City on the Willamette* (Portland, 1952) 16, 21; McArthur, *Oregon Geographic Names*, 600; Turnbull, *History of Oregon Newspapers*, 35-36. In 1850 an "old Oregonian" was anyone who had been in the Pacific Northwest in 1846 and before. Randall V. Mills, "Oregon Speechways," in *American Speech* 25 (1950) 85.

51. Teiser, "Orville Pratt," 177; E. Kimbark MacColl, *Merchants, Money, & Power* (Portland, 1988) 7, 14.

52. Criminal Procedure Acts, *Little Bluebook*, 116, *Big Bluebook*, 155.

53. Historical reports saying that defense counsel were paid with fifty Cayuse horses all stem from the sometimes dubious reminiscences of Joe Meek through his biographer, Frances Fuller Victor, in *River of the West*, 494-95. Concerning the dollar value of a Cayuse horse in 1848, see Bancroft, *Oregon*, 2:44.

54. Criminal Procedure Acts, *Little Bluebook*, 119, *Big Bluebook*, 158.

55. Prosecutor fees for drawing up eight indictments against the Cayuse defendants were $30 to $60 each (*Oregonian*, September 24, 1933). The Snoqualmich murder trial in Puget Sound eight months previously cost more than $1,900, including $500 for lawyers' fees. Bancroft, *Oregon*, 2:80. Victor reported that the Snoqualmich trial cost $4,000. *River of the West*, 501. In the Cayuse trial, one of the defense counsel was paid $500 by the U.S. Government. Drury, *Marcus and Narcissa Whitman*, 2:325. The list of witnesses called by the prosecution and the marshal's costs in serving summonses are in File, *United States v. Telokite*. All of this, and the fact that the court did in fact *appoint* counsel (*Spectator*, May 30, 1850), suggests that the horses remaining after payment of trial costs were insufficient to "procure counsel."

56. 1850 Order Book, Item 12. It was not until Oregon became a state that the legislature required a bar examination as a prerequisite to the practice of law. *General Laws of Oregon*, sec. 1002, 306.

57. *History of Bench and Bar*, 263; MacColl, *Merchants, Money & Power*, 53; Clark, *Eden Seekers*, 251; Teiser, "Orville Pratt," 181.

58. Bancroft, *Oregon*, 2:67, 79-80; *Spectator*, October 18, 1849; Tobie, *No Man Like Joe*, 193-96.

59. *History of Bench and Bar*, 269; Clark, *Eden Seekers*, 250, 270-71; Harry E. Pratt, "22 Letters of David Logan, Pioneer Oregon Lawyer," *OHQ* 44 (1943) 253; *United States v. Tom*, 1 Or. 26 (1853). See text at notes 81-82, infra.

60. *History of Bench and Bar*, 271.

61. Ibid. at 280.

62. Clark, *Eden Seekers*, 228; Victor, *River of the West*, 495.

63. Victor, *River of the West*, 495; Bancroft, *Oregon*, 2:81, 91.

64. *Spectator*, May 30, 1850.

65. A.M.A. Blanchet, *Journal of a Catholic Bishop on the Oregon Trail*, ed. Edward J. Kowrach (Fairfield, Wash., 1978) 115; Osborne Cross, "Journal of Major Osborne Cross," Settle, *Mounted Riflemen*, 262 n.263.

Ironically, Captain Claiborne, who defended the accused Cayuse against what he considered frontier oppression, became a colonel in the Civil War eleven years later on the side of the Confederacy, defending states' rights to continue slavery. Ibid.

66. Attribution of the legal papers to Claiborne's hand is based upon a comparison to Claiborne's signature by this author, who makes no claim to handwriting expertise. Still, the comparison appears unmistakable in view of the peculiarities in Claiborne's penmanship. Concerning the Bill of Exceptions, see note 105, infra, and Appendix A.

67. Victor, *River of the West*, 495; Clark, *Eden Seekers*, 235. The military record on Major Reynolds, the paymaster, is also silent. He is nowhere reported to be an officer in the Mounted Rifle Regiment in the journals of Major Osborne Cross, George Gibb, or Colonel William Loring, all of whom were a part of the regiment's two-thousand-mile trek to Oregon. See Settle, *Mounted Riflemen*.

68. Criminal Procedure Acts, *Little Bluebook*, sec. 69, 117, *Big Bluebook*, sec. 69, 156.

69. Criminal Procedure Acts, *Little Bluebook*, sec. 66, 117, *Big Bluebook*, sec. 66, 155. For the grant of the motion for continuance, see 1850 Order Book, 26.

70. Drury, *Marcus and Narcissa Whitman*, 2:205-65; Thompson, *Shallow Grave*, 92-103. The "Gillon" indictment undoubtedly refers to Isaac Gilliland. Indictment Sixteen is entitled "U.S. v. Frank Escaloom"; there is no indication that a true bill was ever found in this case or that it was connected to the massacre.

Although these six other indictments and true bills were presented to the court, defendants were never arraigned under them. They were all continued, and eventually dismissed a year and a half later by Holbrook under *nolle prosequi* (no prosecution) motions. 1850 Order Book, 33-34, 37-38.

Some say there were *fourteen* massacre victims. These reports include Peter D. Hall, who disappeared after a successful escape to Fort Walla Walla. Drury, *Marcus and Narcissa Whitman*, 2:243. The mass grave naming these fourteen victims may be seen today at the site of the massacre. Thompson, *Shallow Grave*, 132. No indictments were presented for these seven additional victims.

Still other victims include diseased children who died of neglect during the captivity, e.g., the children of Meek and Jim Bridger. Drury, *Marcus and Narcissa Whitman*, 2:260, 299.

71. *Spectator*, January 20, 1848.

72. Clifford M. Drury, "Joe Meek Comments on Reasons for the Whitman Massacre," *OHQ* 75 (1974) 74-75.

73. Contrast the composition of Meek's letters to his son Courtney as quoted in Tobie, *No Man Like Joe*, 260-61.

74. Campbell, *Autobiography*, 232-33, 240-41. See also Victor, *River of the West*, 404, where the test given is explained differently: three Cayuse were taken to Whitman for his care; two were sick, but the third was healthy; all three died following the giving of Whitman's medicines.

75. The Oregon State Archives file in Salem includes two documents, apparently in the same handwriting. One of them is the quoted Plea in Bar and the other is incidentally labeled "demurrer" by an unknown hand. The demurrer does not appear to be officially filed as a court paper. It has essentially the same language as the Plea in Bar except that the demurrer cites to the "Act of Congress of June 30, 1834" for a definition of "Indian Country."

76. Indian Trade and Intercourse Act of 1834, 4 Stat. 729, secs. 1, 25.

77. Concerning the definitions and consequences of designating a district as Indian Country, see Jeff Zucker, Kay Hummel, and Bob Hogfoss, *Oregon Indians: Culture, History and Current Affairs* (Portland, 1983) 82; David H. Getches et al., *Federal Indian Law, Cases and Materials*, 2d ed. (St. Paul, 1986) 338-39; Oliver LaFarge, *Pictorial History of the American Indian* (New York, 1974) 241-42.

78. Concerning the absence of federal government control between August 1846 and August 1848, see Fenton, "Winning of the Oregon Country," 351-52.

79. Article III of the Articles of Compact of 1787 incorporated in the Oregon Territorial Act of 1848 and Article I, sec. 3, Organic Law of the Oregon Provisional Government, in *General Laws of Oregon*, 47, 59.

80. *Spectator*, May 30, 1850; 1850 Order Book, 28; Bancroft, *Oregon*, 2:96. For an explanation of Pratt's reasoning, see Bancroft, *Chronicles of the Builders*, 2:243-44.

81. Act of June 5, 1850, 9 U.S. Stat. at Large.

82. *United States v. Tom.*

83. See text at note 99, infra. H.S. Lyman, "Reminiscences," *QOHS* 4 (1903) 253-54; Drury, *Marcus and Narcissa Whitman*, 2:161.

84. *Spectator*, May 30, 1850.

85. "Diary of Reverend G.H. Atkinson," ed. E. Ruth Rockwood, *OHQ* 41 (1940) 25-26.

86. Ruby and Brown, *The Cayuse*, 171; *Oregonian*, November 19, 1879 (quoting a story from the *Army and Navy Journal*). Bancroft, *Chronicles of the Builders*, 2:243, confirms the defendants' observations about the state of excitement in the populace:

> The possibility that the assassins might escape through some technicality was sufficient to arouse a cry of vengeance throughout the land. Had they been discharged . . . or . . . postponed, they would probably have been hanged, or more likely torn to pieces by an infuriated populace.

87. Oregon Territorial Act, sec. 9, 1848.

88. Essentially, the first and second judicial districts included what are now Oregon and southern Idaho, and the third district included what are now Washington; the Idaho panhandle; parts of western Montana; and Clatsop County, Oregon. Sidney Teiser, "William Strong, Associate Justice of the Territorial Courts," *OHQ* 64 (1963) 293, 296; idem, "Orville Pratt," 178; Donald C. Johnson, "Politics, Personalities, and Policies of the Oregon Territorial Supreme Court," *Environmental Law* 4 (1973) 14; Clark, *Eden Seekers*, 231; *History of Bench and Bar*, 277; Hendrickson, *Joe Lane*, 16.

89. For the location of Waiilatpu on the old Walla Walla River channel, see Drury, *Marcus and Narcissa Whitman*, 1:224-25, 345.

90. See note 70, supra. Victor (Bancroft, *Oregon*, 2:96) reports that the defendants pled not guilty to the Narcissa Whitman and Luke Saunders indictments. The 1850 Order Book (37-38) shows clearly that this is not correct; no pleas were taken.

91. Historians have also struggled with the spelling: "Telaukaikt" (Victor, *River of the West*), "Tilaukait" (Hulbert, *Marcus Whitman, Crusader*; Jones, *The Great Command*), "Tiloukaikt" (Clark, *Eden Seekers*; Drury, *Marcus and Narcissa Whitman*), "Tiloukikt" (Tobie, *No Man Like Joe*), "Toloquwet" (Mary Saunders, *The Whitman Massacre: A True Story by a Survivor* [1916; reprint, Fairfield, Wash., 1977]).

See Drury, *Marcus and Narcissa Whitman*, 2:213-15, for a list of myriad variations on Cayuse names. Without modern techniques for identification (fingerprints, drivers' licenses, Social Security numbers, birth certificates) and with only the dubious method of eyewitness identification, early pioneers and historians had little notion of who was who in the world of the original Americans.

92., *Spectator*, January 20, 1848.

93. The 1850 Order Book says nothing about any motion for continuance. The *Spectator* reported that a continuance was requested and that an "affidavit was filed, which was deemed insufficient." The written request to produce Quishem is in File, *United States v. Telokite*. That request begins with language typical of an affidavit; therefore, the request is probably the affidavit referred to in the *Spectator* article. One may speculate as to the reasons for obscurity in the court record. The denial of a properly filed request to subpoena a witness on the accused's behalf could have been a violation of the Sixth Amendment to the U.S. Constitution: "In all criminal prosecutions, the accused shall enjoy the right . . . to have compulsory process for obtaining witnesses in his favor."

94. Claiborne's penning of the name "Quishem" was undoubtedly a phonetic spelling of what he heard old Chief Telokite say. Phonetically, "Quishem" sounds similar to the name of one of the defendants—Kiamasumkin, whose name was also spelled "Quiahmaysun" and "Quiamashouskin" (Drury, *Marcus and Narcissa Whitman*, 2:215), the latter version lending itself to the shorter sobriquet "Quiamash." Is it possible that the mysterious *Quishem* was a principal in the massacre and that mispronunciations and misspellings caused *Quiamash* (Kiamasumkin) to be confused with *Quishem?*

95. "Jurors" Act, sec. 1, *Little Bluebook*, 277, *Big Bluebook*, 296. And see *Twenty Acts*, 116-17.

Concerning Parrott, see McArthur, *Oregon Geographic Names*, 573, and "Accessions," *QOHS* 6 (1905) 341. Concerning Albion Post, see "Autobiography of Robert Valentine Short," *QOHS* 7 (1906) 54. Concerning the "stranger," see *Oregonian*, November 29, 1879.

96. Tobie, *No Man Like Joe*, "Jurors" Act, sec. 1, *Little Bluebook*, 277, *Big Bluebook*, 296.

97. The procedure was in accord with the *Bluebooks*: "Jurors" Act, sec. 8, and "Courts" Act, sec. 61, *Little Bluebook*, 116, 279; *Big Bluebook*, 155, 298. And see *Twenty Acts*, 118.

98. The details of the questioning of the jury panelists—today called the *voir dire*—does not appear in the historical record. We know, however, that there must have been extensive inquiry. The narrative account is a fair prediction of its probable focus.

99. Lyman, "Reminiscences," 255-56.

100. The *Spectator* (May 30, 1850) reported that there were "twenty persons . . . peremptorily challenged by the Counsel for the Indians, and two by the District Attorney."

The *Bluebooks* authorized the court to draft bystanders when there was not a sufficient number of jurors in attendance. "Jurors" Act, *Little Bluebook*, 280, *Big Bluebook*, 299. And see *Twenty Acts*, 118-19. That bystanders must have been used was evident, because twenty-two challenges would have exhausted the original twenty-four summonsed jury panelists. The conscription of Anson Cone and his cohort bears this out.

With twenty-two challenges and twelve final jurors, thirty-four panelists must have been questioned. Frances Fuller Victor reported that thirty-eight jurymen were called. *Indian Wars of Oregon* (Salem, Oreg., 1894) 250. If the calling, questioning, and challenging of jurors took an average of five minutes each, the entire *voir dire* would have taken almost three hours, including the time for the marshal to conscript enough bystanders to fill out the exhausted supply of twenty-four original jury panelists.

The *Bluebooks* provided that, in a capital case, the defendant "may challenge peremptorily 12 jurors and no more," while the prosecutor "shall have a right to challenge one half as many as the defendant is entitled to." Criminal Procedure Acts, sec. 62, *Little Bluebook*, 116, *Big Bluebook*, 155. By that allowance, it might seem that the defense got more than its fair share of challenges. But with five defendants, a fair allowance of twelve challenges each would have made a total of sixty allowable challenges by the defense and thirty for the prosecution. Needless to say, if both sides had exhausted their ninety challenges, the pool of adult male spectators in the courtroom would have been heavily taxed.

101. These spellings are as they appear to be from the signatures on the verdict form. The 1850 Order Book reports some of the last names as "Parrott" (instead of Parrot); "Alfrey" (instead of Olfrey); "Dennison" (instead of Densmore); "Ellenburg" (instead of Ellenburgh).

102. The *Bluebooks* provided this specific Juror's Oath. "Jurors" Act, sec. 5, *Little Bluebook*, 279, *Big Bluebook*, 298. And see *Twenty Acts*, 118.

103. On September 3, 1849, the Second Session of the Oregon Territorial Legislature passed a statute concerning oath and affirmation. Three forms of oath were provided. One was in the form given in the text. For those who chose not to put their hands on the Bible, but rather to "swear with the hand uplifted," the appropriate words were: "You do solemnly swear. . . . " A third choice was provided for those "who may have conscientious scruples against taking oath" and who could say instead, "You do solemnly, sincerely, and truly, declare and affirm. . . ."

This law was not published until 1851, but Curry would have been aware of it in May 1850. Statutes of a General Nature (December, 1850) 182.

Undoubtedly, Eliza Hall would have chosen the biblical swearing form.

104. Victor, *River of the West*, 494; Bancroft, *Oregon*, 2:95. It may be that some of the testimony was heard in the morning. The Order Book minutes recite that "part of the testimony" was heard before the noon recess. The timing of that recess, as reported in the narrative, is a surmise based upon an assumption that the process of selecting the jury would have taken almost three hours. That assumed length of time for jury selection may be too generous. It is possible that the noon recess was called somewhere later on in Mrs. Hall's testimony.

105. The "verbatim" narration of the testimony in the text is fictional only because it invents the dialogue. It is, however, real in the sense that it attempts to restore the contemporaneous summaries to their original luster.

The Bill of Exceptions was a *summary* transcript. It is quoted in full in Appendix A. *Verbatim* transcribing of trials was simply not done in 1850. There were no court reporters. The first known official shorthand reporter in Oregon Country was Thomas H. Pearne. He kept a record of the State Constitutional Convention, but that did not happen until seven years after the trial. Geer, *Fifty Years in Oregon*, 97.

For purpose of appellate review, a summary transcript of witness testimony was prepared by the party seeking appeal. This summary became part of the Bill of Exceptions. In two of the first reported opinions of the Oregon Territorial Supreme Court, the court made clear that the Bill of Exceptions was an absolute requirement for appeal. *Thompson v. Backenstos*, 1 Ore. 17 (1853); *Scott v. Cook*, 1 Ore. 24 (1853). See also *Twenty Acts*, Practice Chapter, sec. 19, p. 124.

The Bill of Exceptions, initially prepared by an advocate, was subject to the trial judge's amendments. In the Cayuse trial, Judge Pratt made several written amendments to defense counsels' summary of the testimony. Those amendments are quoted in full in Appendix B. It was the law in 1850 that the Bill of Exceptions, as amended by the trial judge, uncontested by opposing counsel, had to be accepted as a true summary of the testimony, at least for appellate purposes. Burr W. Jones, *Law of Evidence*, 2d ed. (San Francisco, 1896) 426.

There have been other dramatized accounts of what occurred at the Cayuse trial (e.g., Don Berry's novel *Moontrap* [New York, 1962] 122 *et seq.)* and other cursory accounts (e.g., Ruby and Brown, *The Cayuse*, 164-68). But the amended Bill of Exceptions and the *Spectator* news article (Appendix C) are the only two contemporaneous records of the witnesses' testimony.

106. The answers up to this point do not appear in the Bill of Exceptions or the *Spectator* article, but they are documented by other research. They are here sim-

ply to provide preliminary perspective. Drury, *Marcus and Narcissa Whitman*, 2:202, 241-43; Thompson, *Shallow Grave*, 64; Eells, *Marcus Whitman, Pathfinder and Patriot*, 101. See also the archaeological discoveries at the Whitman Mission National Historic Site.

107. There is no indication in the Bill of Exceptions or *Spectator* article that this or any other in-court identifications were ever made. It is reported here because it is unlikely that Holbrook would have neglected that kind of fundamental trial practice.

108. Tomsucky was reportedly shot and probably killed in the two-year pursuit of the Cayuse that preceded the trial. Drury, *Marcus and Narcissa Whitman*, 2:323.

109. We may assume that the expression "throw up his hands" meant that Rogers was struck by gunfire. Indeed, we know from other secondary sources that he was killed then. Thompson, *Shallow Grave*, 99; Drury, *Marcus and Narcissa Whitman*, 2:237.

110. The primary sources do not separate the witnesses' testimony between direct questioning and cross-examination. The narrative's allocation of questioning between the prosecution and the defense is a surmise based upon which side probably sought to elicit which information.

111. Catherine and Elizabeth Sager, ages thirteen and ten years respectively at the time of the massacre, were present at the Mission House at the time of the attack on Marcus Whitman. Both reported in their later years that Whitman was accosted in the kitchen inside the Mission House. What witness Hall probably saw was the assault on Luke Saunders. Drury, *Marcus and Narcissa Whitman*, 2:229-30.

On the other hand, the Sager sisters did not see the assault on Doctor Whitman. Mary Bridger and John Sager were reportedly the only ones present at the time in the kitchen, where it is generally agreed that Marcus Whitman was killed; both of them were dead by the time of the trial. Ibid., 299, 234, 225. Thus there were no eyewitnesses of Marcus Whitman's killing other than Mrs. Hall, who swore that she saw (from a distance of a hundred obstructed yards) that the assault occurred outdoors and that it was made by Telokite.

At the archaeological site of Waiilatpu, a rough measurement taken by this author in 1989 showed the distance between the Mansion House and the Mission House as having been more like 120 to 140 yards.

112. Two portraits in the OHS Photograph Collection, File 274, bear the captions "Mrs Rebecca (Hall) (Hopkins) Cone . . . married Anson Cone" and "Anson S. Cone . . . married Rebecca (Hall) Hopkins, a survivor of Whitman massacre." But this casual reference is probably in error. Rebecca's first husband was Philander Johnson Cone, not Anson. H.S. Lyman, "Reminiscences," *QOHS* 4 (1903) 259.

113. Thompson, *Shallow Grave*, 23-42, 138.

114. The door referred to here is probably a door between the kitchen and sitting room inside the Mission House. Drury, *Marcus and Narcissa Whitman*, 2:225.

115. In fact, both of her brothers, Francis and John, were killed that day. Ibid., 226, 234.

116. The record does not show the witness's response to this obvious point of clarification. The Bill of Exceptions states that Elizabeth Sager testified that Lewis said "he intended to tell the Indians to kill him the said *Jo Lewis*." This is undoubtedly an erroneous transcript or misunderstanding. The *Spectator* article makes no mention of this line of inquiry. All secondary sources make it absolutely clear that Joe Lewis—a half-breed—was a firebrand who had prompted the Cayuse to kill Whitman. Drury, *Marcus and Narcissa Whitman*, 2:212.

117. In the decades following the trial, Elizabeth Sager and her sister Catherine had much more to tell about the massacre than is revealed in the Bill of Exceptions and the *Spectator* article. Unlike the first witness, Eliza Hall, Elizabeth gave many recorded accounts of what she experienced at age ten. She was called upon throughout the rest of her life to recite the details of this historical episode. Her accounts ranged from 1855 (when she was eighteen) to 1923 (when she was eighty-six). Elizabeth Sager to Frederick Sager, in the *Oregonian*, October 30, 1932; in Myra Sager Helm, *Lorinda Bewley and the Whitman Massacre* (Portland, 1951) 82, and in various other sources. Elizabeth Sager Helm, interview with Fred Lockley, July 25, 1923, in Fred Lockley, *Oregon Trail Blazers* (New York, 1929) 369 and in idem, *Conversations With Pioneer Women*, comp. and ed. Mike Helm (Eugene, 1981) 44. And see Drury, *Marcus and Narcissa Whitman*, 2:388.

118. Thompson, *Shallow Grave*, 108-10; Helm, *Lorinda Bewley*, 17-18. For some insights into the taboos concerning women, including pregnancy, childbirth, and menstruation, see *Women's Diaries of Westward Journey*, coll. Lillian Schlissel (New York, 1982) 82, 98-99, 106-11. The witness's husband is not to be confused with the lawyer William W. Chapman. See OHS Photograph Collection, File 234.

Of course, the clothing worn by the witnesses is not mentioned in the trial record. The narrative's comments on dress are based upon the reminiscences of pioneer George H. Himes about the attire of those times. See Himes to Karl Onthank, January 26, 1917, in K. Keith Richard, "Of Gingham, Barn Doors, and Exquisites: George H. Himes on Pioneer Fashion," *OHQ* 90 (1989) 387.

119. See text at notes 175-78, infra.

120. This time does not appear in the *Spectator* article or Bill of Exceptions, but was recorded in the witness's deposition taken on December 12, 1848. See Gray, *History of Oregon*, 486.

121. The *Spectator* article uses the word "rehearse." The Bill of Exceptions uses the word "interpreter." Apparently Telokite understood enough English to act as an interpreter for Whitman. The two had frequently "rehearsed" the doctor's sermons before Whitman delivered them to the rest of the tribe. See Ruby and Brown, *Indians*, 77.

122. This is the language of the *Spectator* article and may have been Chapman's. It is not reported in the Bill of Exceptions. It may reasonably be interpreted to mean that the witness was frozen in place by the alarming violence that confronted her.

123. It is in this language that the Bill of Exceptions records the deaths of two more persons. But it is not likely that the witness, Lorinda Chapman, stated it so unfeelingly, because one of those two victims was her brother, Crocket Bewley. Drury, *Marcus and Narcissa Whitman*, 2:263-64.

124. The Osborne family's escape is told in ibid., 247-52.

125. Again, it was Judge Pratt's amendments to the Bill of Exceptions that insisted on the inclusion of the italicized words. See Appendix B.

126. The *Spectator* article reports that Osborne testified that he was sick. That may be incorrect. It was his wife who was sick. It is true, however, that the Osborne family (three children) lived in the Mission House as regular occupants, not in the Mansion House as immigrants. Drury, *Marcus and Narcissa Whitman*, 2:202, 224, 247.

127. See text at note 35, supra.

128. Osborne had been building a floor in one of the Mission House rooms and had not yet nailed some of the boards, under which he hid himself, his wife, and his children. See Osborne to "Dear Brother and Sister," April 7, 1848, the earliest known written report by a survivor of what occurred at the massacre, in Hulbert, *Marcus Whitman, Crusader*, 8:257, 262. And see Drury, *Marcus and Narcissa Whitman*, 2:232.

129. The "young man" was probably Francis Sager. Drury, *Marcus and Narcissa Whitman*, 2:234.

130. The *Spectator* article reports this last piece of testimony concerning Whitman's race and citizenship, but the Bill of Exceptions does not. Nothing in theory or formal law at that time provided for such distinctions; but no one can deny the caste discriminations of that day and age.

131. Drury, *Marcus and Narcissa Whitman*, 2:196, 251-52; Osborne to "Dear Brother and Sister," April 7, 1848, in Hulbert, *Marcus Whitman, Crusader*, 8:257; Thompson, *Shallow Grave*, 89-92.

132. Saunders, *Whitman Massacre*, 17; Thompson, *Shallow Grave*, 90; Drury, *Marcus and Narcissa Whitman*, 2:200.

133. Many of these were captive survivors of the mission massacre. Some were Indians whose identities are lost in history. One of them was probably "Beardy," a Cayuse chief who had aided the survivors in captivity. Catherine Sager Pringle, "Christmas with the Whitman Captives 1847," ed. Henry M. Majors, *Northwest Discovery* 1 (December 1980) 361-64; Drury, *Marcus and Narcissa Whitman*, 2:238-39. Peter Skene Ogden was chief factor at Fort Vancouver for the Hudson's Bay Company. It was he who arranged for the release of the white survivors after one month of captivity. Ibid. at 288.

134. *Spectator*, May 16, 1850.

135. *Ladies' Home Journal* (August 1913) 14, 40. Eliza was probably speaking about her grand jury testimony because both the *Spectator* article and the Bill of Exceptions clearly show that she did not testify at trial before the petit jury. Nevertheless, her statement is troublesome because, today at least, defendants are not allowed to be present in grand jury proceedings. This modern rule may have been relaxed in the Cayuse capital murder case.

Equally troublesome is the reminiscence of petit juryman J.T. Hunsaker, who indirectly alludes to Eliza Spalding's testimony. See note 169, infra. But he, too, may have been referring to her grand jury testimony or private conversations.

136. *Ladies' Home Journal* (August 1913) 14.

137. Drury, *Marcus and Narcissa Whitman* 2:388 (listing two major accounts by Catherine Sager); Catherine Sager Pringle, "Seven Orphans on the Oregon Trail," ed. Henry M. Majors, *Northwest Discovery* 1 (December 1980) 314.

138. Saunders, *Whitman Massacre*, a reprint of a 1916 booklet printed in Oakland, California. This booklet says that it has been "arranged for publication by Phoebe L. Saunders McKay," Mary Saunders's daughter who also survived the massacre. A handwritten deposition, signed and sworn to by "Mrs. Husted formerly Mrs. Saunders" on July 1, 1884, on file at the Whitman Mission National Historic Site, is the only discovered document showing that Husted and Saunders were the same person. The published booklet does not make this connection, nor do the trial records. Although the booklet and the deposition seem to follow the same substantive story line, the words and form clearly differ. For this reason, it seems fair to conclude that the 1916 booklet was actually written by Phoebe Saunders McKay, relying heavily upon her mother's 1884 deposition.

139. Ibid. at 35; Drury, *Marcus and Narcissa Whitman*, 1:267, 2:272; Sara Hunsaker (daughter of juryman J.T. Hunsaker) to her grandchildren, September 15, 1930 (see note 169, infra).

140. Elam Young was presumably at the trial or at least in the vicinity during the trial. Two months after the trial he wrote a letter from the nearby Twality Plains criticizing Judge Pratt's morals. See text at note 32, supra.

141. Thompson, *Shallow Grave*, 110; Saunders, *Whitman Massacre*, 40-41.

142. Richard, "Gingham, Barn Doors, and Exquisites," 389-92.

143. *History of Bench and Bar*, 12.

144. Four months after the trial, Congress passed the Donation Land Claim Act of 1850 (9 Stat. 497), which effectively disowned McLoughlin of certain of his land claims in the Oregon City area. *General Laws of Oregon*, sec. 11, 68. See also Sidney Teiser, "The First Chief Justice of Oregon Territory: William P. Bryant," *OHQ* 48 (1947) 45; Johnson, "Politics, Personalities and Policies," 14. And see *Reader's Encyclopedia of the American West*, s.v. "McLoughlin, John."

145. Clark, *Eden Seekers*, 155. Jones, *The Great Command*, 143; Eva Emery Dye, *McLoughlin and Old Oregon: A Chronicle* (Chicago, 1900) 1-39. None of the foregoing preliminary questioning appears in the Bill of Exceptions or the *Spectator* article. But it is hard to believe that the defense, having called as prominent a figure as McLoughlin, would not have taken the time to explore some of his credentials and his loyalties to the new American government.

The record does not indicate which of the three defense lawyers conducted the examination of witnesses. The conclusion that Pritchette conducted the interrogations, especially the questioning of a prestigious witness like McLoughlin, is based on the fact that Pritchette was the territorial secretary and the only trained lawyer of the three.

146. While the *Spectator* article and the Bill of Exceptions at this point do not indicate it, McLoughlin probably explained that the Cayuse practice was to kill only *bad* medicine men, i.e., those who were ineffective in treating the sick. This practice was borne out by Overton Johnson and William H. Winters in an account of their travels in the West:

> These Medicine-men are supposed to be invulnerable. . . .
> They are held accountable for the success of anything which
> they undertake, and if a person dies in their hands, or if they
> lose an engagement, they are tried for their lives. ("Route
> Across the Rocky Mountains with a Description of Oregon and
> California, 1843" [1846; reprint, *QOHS* 7 (1906) 181].)

It is possible that McLoughlin was mistaken as to the years of his warnings. In 1840 and 1841 there did not appear to be any major Indian problems at the mission. But in later years, white migration and the spread of disease began to increase, so that by 1845 McLoughlin's warnings to Whitman can be documented. Drury, *Marcus and Narcissa Whitman*, 2:135. In any case, warnings to Whitman were probably unnecessary, because, as far back as 1837, the Whitmans knew from firsthand experience that the Cayuse killed ineffective medicine men (*tewats*). In that year, Narcissa wrote that a *tewat* was shot and killed by a Cayuse because the *tewat* allowed a relative to die of sickness. Narcissa Whitman to Stephen and Clarissa Prentiss, March 30, 1837, *Transactions of the Oregon Pioneer Association, 1891*.

147. Clark, *Eden Seekers*, 174-77.

148. *Twenty Acts*, Practice Chapter, sec. 37, 127.

149. Drury, *Marcus and Narcissa Whitman*, 1:251-52, 2:83; S.A. Clarke, *Pioneer Days of Oregon History*, 2 vols. (Portland, 1905) 1:568; Thompson, *Shallow Grave*, 92.

150. See note 103, supra, for the various forms of "swearing" a witness.

That Stickus was not given oath or affirmation is a conclusion taken from the *Spectator* article (Appendix C). That article separately recites that each of the six other witnesses was "sworn." Conspicuously, no such recital is made concerning Stickus; in place thereof, the paragraph on him contains a parenthetical recital: "(a Cayuse Indian)."

151. The *Spectator* reported this last piece of testimony, but the defendants' Bill of Exceptions did not. The omission fortifies the fact that it was not good testimony for the defendants, because it supports the elements of conspiracy and premeditation—Tomsucky being one of the Cayuse involved in the massacre, albeit not here charged. But if the testimony had been offered by the prosecution for this latter purpose, without more foundation laid, it should have been inadmissible hearsay had the defense lawyers objected, which they did not.

The narrative takes some liberty in reporting the *Spectator*'s and Bill of Exception's accounts of the testimony of Stickus; the narrative translates those accounts into what would be Native American diction and vernacular—in this case the language is Chinook Jargon, not Cayuse-Nez Perce. As of 1843, Chief Stickus could not understand or speak English. Geer, *Fifty Years in Oregon*, 157-58.

152. See the series of articles by Spalding and Griffin in the *Oregon American and Evangelical Unionist*, July 1848-May 1849, in OHS Ms. 1203. And see Gray, *History of Oregon*.

See generally Clark, *Eden Seekers*, 216-17, 238; *Reader's Encyclopedia of the American West*, s.v. "Spalding, Henry."

153. See text at note 64, supra.

154. The *Spectator* article (Appendix C) reports that Spalding was a witness, while the Bill of Exceptions (Appendix A) makes no mention of this. Atkinson, in his "Diary," records that Spalding was *summonsed* as a witness. Knowing how Captain Claiborne felt about Spalding, it is entirely possible that Claiborne left Spalding's testimony out of the Bill of Exceptions as a deliberate slight.

155. Other reports show that Spalding had left *two* days, not one day, after the massacre. Whitman had left the Stickus lodge on Sunday evening. The massacre at Waiilatpu occurred on Monday afternoon. Spalding left the Umatilla River for his own mission at Lapwai on Wednesday. Drury, *Marcus and Narcissa Whitman*, 2:221-22, 253.

156. The *Spectator* newspaper article records, "There the testimony closed." The Bill of Exceptions records, "This was all the evidence given in the cause." Thus, these primary authorities confirm that no other witnesses were called.

157. It is here that a discrepancy occurs in the *Spectator* article and the 1850 Order Book (30). The Order Book reports that some testimony was heard on the next day, Friday morning. This would mean that final arguments of counsel must have been made on Friday. But the *Spectator* article reports that they were made on Thursday. The newspaper is explicit and detailed about the final arguments' having been held on Thursday, whereas the Order Book never mentions final arguments. Our narrative text follows the timing laid down in the *Spectator*'s "minute and faithful" reporting.

Accordingly, it is likely that Judge Pratt would have called a short recess at this point, and not an adjournment.

158. Perkins to Jane Prentiss, October 19, 1849, in Drury, *Marcus and Narcissa Whitman*, 2:390. Judge William Strong's opinion of Narcissa confirms Perkins's assessment: "She could not bear to have the filthy Indians around. She had a natural repugnance to the filthy, dirty, lazy Indians; almost everybody has. Most Indians do not like that." "Knickerbocker Views of the Oregon Country," *OHQ* 62 (1961) 77. It should be noted, however, that while both Perkins and Strong were personally acquainted with Narcissa Whitman, the severity of their assessments must be tempered by the fact that neither of them had seen her with the Cayuse at Waiilatpu.

159. *Spectator*, May 30, 1850; Victor, *River of the West*, 495.

160. 1850 Order Book, 30.

161. The extreme length of that eventful court day (Thursday, May 23, 1850) is based upon the author's following time estimates:

Court Convened	9:00 A.M.
Motion for Continuance (approx. 15 min.)	9:00-9:15 A.M.
Selection of Jury and Opening Statement	
(almost 3 hrs.)	9:15 A.M.-12:00 P.M.
Lunch Break	12:00-2:00 P.M.
Testimony of 7 Witnesses	
(avg. 15 min. ea. plus recess)	2:00-4:00 P.M.
Closing Arguments	
(as reported by *Spectator*: 3 hours)	4:00-7:00 P.M.

162. The state of Idaho takes its name from the Cayuse-Nez Perce word *Edahoe*, meaning "light on the mountains." Gwendolen Gishler and Pearl Hayden, *Thunderhill* (Portland, 1947) 5.

163. See note 171, infra.

164. We may safely assume that the two direct and contemporaneous trial reports, being mere summaries and non-verbatim, would necessarily leave some testimony unreported. But counsel for the defendants, in preparing the Bill of Exceptions, Judge Pratt in amending it, and the *Spectator* journalist, in faithfully reporting "the most material points to which witnesses testified," certainly would have recorded most, if not all, eyewitness identifications of, and crime perpetrations by, the specific defendants on trial. Our narrative text, therefore, would seem to be a reliable summary of the testimonial identifications. Accordingly, many commentators opine that Kiamasumkin was probably innocent. E.g., Drury, *Marcus and Narcissa Whitman*, 2:329. We can never really know if he was innocent *in fact*, even though it seems safe to say that he should have been innocent *in the eyes of the law*.

165. File, *United States v. Telokite*, Motion for New Trial. The narrator's observations about hearsay and confrontation do not appear in the record, but may fairly be implied from defense counsel's stated objections. Today, Judge Pratt's actions would have been a clear violation of the hearsay rule and the U.S. Constitution's Sixth Amendment confrontation clause: "the accused shall enjoy the right .. to be confronted with the witnesses against him." In 1859 the Oregon State Constitution would express that same right in these terms: "The accused shall have the right . . . to meet the witnesses face to face." Article I, sec. 11.

166. Victor, *River of the West*, 494; Bancroft, *Oregon*, 2:95.

167. Drury, *Marcus and Narcissa Whitman*, 2:324.

168. Ironically, Marcus Whitman himself had proposed to Congress in 1843 that criminal Indians ("savages") be tried by their own tribe, rather than by "distant tribunals," and then be surrendered to the white man for punishment, the surrender constituting proof of guilt. Whitman to the Secretary of War (undated) with a "Proposed Bill," ibid. at 2:397-98, 400.

169. The Hunsaker revelations about the jury deliberations and his own misgivings are in a letter written by Sara Hunsaker Tompkins to "My dear grandchildren" on September 15, 1930. Sara Hunsaker was the daughter of juryman J.T. Hunsaker. The original of this letter is in the possession of Kathleen Reierson, Condon, Oregon. A typed copy of the letter, as yet uncatalogued, is at the Oregon Historical Society. Pertinent excerpts are here quoted:

> The [1846] wagon train was guided many weeks by an Indian sent by Marcus Whitman from his mission. He showed such kindness, was so friendly to the emigrants that he completely won the friendship of my father. This same Indian, in after years, was among the Indians being tried for murder at the Whitman Massacre. My father was on the jury. . . . [F]ather was not satisfied with the testimony against him. He said if the witness had given her testimony against him in the same serious way Eliza Spaulding did, as though she thought an Indian was

> a human being, he would not have questioned it. As it was he
> could not at first agree to hang that Indian, so he did what they
> called then, 'hung the jury.' When the jury could not agree . . . ,
> they shut them up, fed them on a light diet until they did agree.
> Father told me the other jurors all agreed that this Indian was
> guilty. He alone was disagreeing. The eleven other jurors told
> him the evidence was against the Indian that they were all
> needed at home. . . . After a time he yielded to agree . . . ,
> thought [though] he did not like the light-hearted way the testi-
> mony was given. Father told me many years after that he
> wished he never had agreed to call that Indian guilty—he could
> not help but doubt.

The contents of the letter do not identify the Indian in question. That it was Kiamasumkin is conjecture based upon the observation that the evidence against
him was the weakest. See note 164, supra.

170. The 1850 Order Book (30) states: "After a short absence, [the jury] returned
into court for the purpose of clearing some misunderstanding and after having
heard the witness again returned to consider of their presentments." The Order
Book does not indicate who the witness was or what misunderstanding needed
clarification. That the witness was Chapman is a conjecture based upon Pratt's
amendments to the Bill of Exceptions and upon an article in the *Oregonian*, dated
November 29, 1879:

> [T]here was some doubt as to the guilt of one of them, as the
> evidence that he did any killing was not conclusive, but it was
> proven that he was present and armed at the time and accord-
> ing to the instructions of the judge the one unwilling juror was
> obliged to render a verdict of guilty against him as well.

Chapman may not have given *new* testimony, but may simply have *reiterated* her
former testimony. Today, the practice of hearing further testimony after the close
of the prosecutor's case would be disallowed. But in 1850 the practice may have
been an expedient tolerated when no verbatim record was kept and clarification of former testimony was needed.

171. While the deliberations apparently lasted only one hour and fifteen minutes, juryman Hunsaker's reminiscences (note 169, supra) suggest a more prolonged debate over Kiamasumkin's innocence. This discrepancy may be recon-
ciled by the likelihood that the jurors had improperly begun their discussions
while sequestered the night before.

172. *Spectator*, June 11, 1846; *Oregon Journal*, November 8 and 11, 1935.

173. "Verdict," File, *United States v. Telokite*, May 24, 1850.

174. Bancroft, *Oregon*, 2:97.

175. While the *Spectator* article and the Bill of Exceptions show that two separate
motions were made, they do not indicate that it was Claiborne and Pritchette,
respectively, who advanced the motions. The narrator's observations of author-

ship are predicated on the fact that the Motion in Arrest of Judgment was not formalized, whereas the Motion for New Trial was in written form and signed by the *X* marks of each of the defendants. Because that written motion was filed so soon after the verdict was rendered, someone must have anticipated a Guilty finding. It is more likely that Pritchette, the experienced lawyer, would have been so prepared.

The Order Book suggests that the prisoners were taken back to the jail and were not present when either of these motions was made.

176. The Territorial Act of Congress defined the Oregon Territory as bordered on the east by the Rocky Mountains, on the west by the Pacific Ocean, on the north by the forty-ninth parallel (Canadian border), and the south by the forty-second parallel (California border). Waiilatpu was five miles north of the forty-sixth parallel and midway between the Rockies and the Pacific. 9 Stat. 323, sec. 1 (1849).

177. In today's courts, it is permissible in a criminal case to take judicial notice of a fact not reasonably disputable and to allow a jury to infer such a fact without the necessity for proof. (Federal Rule of Evidence 201.) Geographical locations within borders are classic examples of such judicial notice. E.g., *State v. Willard*, 96 Or. App. 219, 772 P.2d 948 (1989). And see Jones, *Law of Evidence*, secs. 107, 127.

178. See text at note 119, supra.

179. Teiser, "Orville Pratt," 178-79; Johnson, "Pioneer Court 1849-59," 29. The third judge was William Strong, an easterner. At the time of trial he had been appointed, but the long trip from east to west meant that he would not arrive in Oregon with news of his appointment until late August. Teiser, "William Strong," 295.

180. 9 Stat. 323, sec. 9 (1849), *General Laws of Oregon*, 56.

181. *Ex Parte Crow Dog*, 109 U.S. 571 (1883). In that case, the Supreme Court of the United States held that a federal district court did not have jurisdiction over the murder of one Indian by another on an Indian reservation.

182. See text at notes 194-95, infra, for Pritchette's other plan.

Defense counsel could have insisted on judicial review by the Supreme Court of the United States—the next high court. It is doubtful that the U.S. Supreme Court would have rejected direct appeal of a district court's proceedings merely because it was not first reviewed by a nonexistent intermediate court of review. Furthermore, if direct appeal to the U.S. Supreme Court was not legally appropriate, defense counsel could have sought a writ of habeas corpus with that august body. U.S. Constitution, Article I, sec. 9. There were potential constitutional errors at trial, e.g., lack of jurisdiction, denial of compulsory process, and denial of the confrontation of witnesses.

Nevertheless, review of the Cayuse trial by the U.S. Supreme Court presented horrendous practical problems that would have taxed any legal system of that day and age. Without benefit of today's travel and communication, an attempted review by a court three thousand miles distant, even if denied, would have delayed the proceedings for years. There were no prisons in the Territory sufficient for such prolonged incarceration. Bancroft, *Chronicles of the Builders*, 2:244.

In view of this dilemma, it is possible that the prayer for an appeal was withdrawn by the defense rather than denied by Pratt. It may have been an expediency by mutual agreement, with which defense counsel simply had to live and by which their clients had to die. See Appendix D for a list of rulings made by the trial judge that might have been potential grounds for a reversal of the conviction on appellate review.

183. The court sentence is a quote taken from the *Spectator* article of May 30, 1850. It is substantially the same as that set forth in the 1850 Order Book (32), except that the Order Book says nothing of the invocation to the grace of God.

184. Atkinson, "Diary," entry for May 24, 1850. See also *Spectator*, May 30, 1850.

185. Hendrickson, *Joe Lane*, 16.

186. Victor, *Early Indian Wars*, 257.

187. Victor reported that the warrant was issued by Governor Lane. *River of the West*, 496; Bancroft, *Oregon*, 2:98 (the original version). The 1850 Order Book (32) reports that the death warrant was issued by the court, which is the customary way of promulgating a death sentence. See Criminal Code of 1864, in *General Laws of Oregon*, 368-69. And see Bancroft, *Oregon*, 2:98, n.69 (the revised version). For the difference between the original and revised versions of this volume, see note 188, infra.

188. The material in this and the two subsequent quotes attributed to Luke Allen is to be found in a revised version of Bancroft, *Oregon*, 2:97-98. The revised version, just like the original, has the same title, publisher, and year of print. Nothing in the revision shows that it is a second edition or a later reprint. Curiously, the original version does not contain the quoted material. Victor, the author of the original version (see note 2, supra), had written this instead at pages 97-98:

> It was predetermined by the people that these Indians should die. . . . There was not the slightest danger that Pratt would go against the people in this matter. . . . He well knew the country would be too hot to hold him should he do otherwise.

Unhappy with Victor's account of the trial, General Lucius H. Allen submitted written corrections to Bancroft. Matthew P. Deady's diary entry for March 2, 1889, reads:

> Got a corrected copy of 2 *Oregon* from Bancroft yesterday, in which I see that there is a new account of the trial of the alleged Whitman murderers before Judge Pratt, said to have been dictated by Gen. Lucius Allen of Allen & Lewis who was in Oregon at the time, and which treats the subject in a much more dignified and complimentary way than the original. (*Pharisee Among Philistines*, 551.)

The reason for the discrepancy in the two printings may be attributed to the business-marketing savvy of the highly successful publisher Hubert Howe Bancroft.

Bancroft's biographer, John W. Caughey, has commented on his subject's "discrepancies":

> There are instances of textual variations for the sake of
> gaining a single customer. For example, the first printing of
> the *History of Oregon* carried a skeptical and unflattering
> account of Judge O.C. Pratt's conduct of the trial. . . . In a
> later printing this account was revised and made much less
> uncomplimentary to the judge. The impulse behind this
> change appears to have been . . . that the judge was giving
> favorable consideration to commissioning Bancroft to do his
> biography. (*Hubert Howe Bancroft*, 296-97.)

Bancroft, *Chronicles of the Builders*, 2:232. See note 32, supra.

It is believed, therefore, that General Allen was the principal author of the revised version of the massacre trial in Bancroft's *History of Oregon*. Bancroft's footnote at page 97 of the revision bears this out: "General Lucius H. Allen, . . . a man of high character, dictated . . . for my use the full particulars of this interesting trial." See also Bancroft, *Chronicles of the Builders*, 2:244-45.

189. Drury, *Marcus and Narcissa Whitman*, 2:327.

190. *Spectator*, May 30, 1850.

191. Sergeant Henry R. Crawford and Corporal Robert D. Mahon, "Important Declaration made June 2d and 3d, 1850," said to be a transcript of the defendants' words, *OHS* Ms. 1203, photocopy; Drury, *Marcus and Narcissa Whitman*, 2:328; Bancroft, *Oregon*, 2:98, n.66.

192. Campbell, *Autobiography*, 242-43.

193. F.N. Blanchet, *Historical Sketches of the Catholic Church in Oregon, During the Past Forty Years* (Portland, 1878) 181; Drury, *Marcus and Narcissa Whitman*, 2:330-31; Bancroft, *Oregon*, 2:99.

194. Tobie, *No Man Like Joe*, 200-201.

195. Clark, *Eden Seekers*, 236; Victor, *Early Indian Wars*, 251; Bancroft, *Oregon*, 2:97 (the revised version). See Oregon Territorial Act, 9 Stat. 323, sec. 3 (1848), in *General Laws of Oregon*, 53.

196. Victor, *Early Indian Wars*, 257-58. Concerning the signator of the warrant (Governor Lane or Judge Pratt), see note 187, supra.

197. Atkinson, "Diary," entry for June 5, 1850; Tobie, *No Man Like Joe*, 201, 303 n.37; Lockley, *Conversations*, 10, 116, 229.

198. Bancroft, *Oregon*, 2:99.

199. See text at note 9, supra.

200. The observation made in the narrative is deduced from a letter by Pritchette to former Provisional Governor Abernethy, dated Sunday, May 26, 1850. Pritchette wrote that the "Chiefs of the Cayuse Nation . . . have become impatient to return to their peoples. . . . [I]n the absence of the Governor, I should take some action in the matter." OHS Ms. 929. The free Cayuse were not in fact present at the

hanging. Drury, *Marcus and Narcissa Whitman*, 2:331. On the other hand, Samuel L. Campbell, who was present at the execution, recalled that Chief Stickus was also present. Idem, *Autobiography*, 243.

201. The story of the execution is gleaned from various accounts: Tobie, *No Man Like Joe*, 201; Lyman, "Reminiscences of John T. Cox," OHS Ms. 722; Victor, *River of the West*, 495-96; Drury, *Marcus and Narcissa Whitman*, 2:331; Lockley, *Conversations*, 10, 116; Bancroft, *Oregon*, 2:97-98 (revised version); Atkinson, "Diary," 26; Lane to Secretary of War, OHS Ms. 1146, Box 5, vol. 5; *Oregonian*, September 24, 1933; Campbell, *Autobiography*, 52, 243; Saunders, *Whitman Massacre*, 26-27; Ruby and Brown, *The Cayuse*, 169-71; *Catholic Sentinel*, April 20, 1872.

202. Victor, *River of the West*, 321.

203. Two sources verify this general location of the unmarked grave: Mr. Hackett and Mrs. Munnick. Today, that location would be somewhere in the vicinity of Kelly Field, in the north part of Oregon City. See *Oregonian*, September 24, 1933; Drury, *Marcus and Narcissa Whitman*, 2:331.

204. *Spectator*, June 13 and 27, 1850.

205. *New York Daily Tribune*, July 8, 1850, reporting an article from the *Sacramento Transcript*, May 29, 1850.

206. *New York Daily Tribune*, August 21, 1850.

207. Letter from "Oregon City, O.T.," May 25, 1850, OHS Ms. 1146, Box 5, vol. 5.

208. Thompson, *Shallow Grave*, 166, n.201.

209. Bancroft, *Oregon*, 2:99.